TRAVELLERS

AMSTERDAM

By
CHRISTOPHER CATLING

Written by Christopher Catling, updated by Joan Gannij
Original photography by Ken Paterson

Published by Thomas Cook Publishing
A division of Thomas Cook Tour Operations Ltd
Company registration no. 1450464 England
The Thomas Cook Business Park, 9 Coningsby Road,
Peterborough PE3 8SB, United Kingdom
E-mail: sales@thomascook.com, Tel: +44 (0) 1733 416477
www.thomascookpublishing.com

Produced by Cambridge Publishing Management Limited
Burr Elm Court, Main Street, Caldecote CB23 7NU

ISBN: 978-1-84157-841-5

Series Editor: Maisie Fitzpatrick
Production/DTP: Steven Collins

Printed and bound in Italy by Printer Trento

Cover photography: Front L-C-R: © Paul Hardy/Corbis; © Pictures Colour
Library; © Damm Stefan/SIME-4Corners Images. Back L-R: © Thomas Cook;
© Ripani Massimo/SIME-4Corners Images.

FSC
Mixed Sources
Product group from well-managed
forests and recycled wood or fibre

Cert no. CQ-COC-000012
www.fsc.org
© 1996 Forest Stewardship Council

Contents

KEY TO MAPS

✈ Airport

★ Start of walk

Ⓜ Metro

Introduction

Samuel Johnson said that anyone who tires of London must be weary of life itself. The same is true of Amsterdam: a seductive and entertaining city made all the more attractive by its manageable size and easy-going atmosphere, Amsterdam combines big city attractions with the character of an overgrown village.

Packed into an area small enough to cross on foot in under half an hour are some 50 museums, over 25 theatres and over 50 art galleries. The city is home to two internationally renowned orchestras, as well as the Dutch national ballet and opera companies. Yet it has none of the stress, hype or tension of a big metropolis: bicycles are more numerous than cars, there are scores of congenial cafés where even first-time visitors are welcomed as old friends and (with the exception of brash Kalverstraat) you will search hard to find a supermarket or chain store – Amsterdammers far prefer their traditional corner-shop grocery stores and specialist retailers.

Above all, Amsterdam is a lived-in city, not one devoted solely to tourism or commerce; after 5pm, when businesses close for the day, the streets throng with Amsterdammers, born and bred in the city, out for a walk or drinking with friends in pavement cafés, lending the city an almost Mediterranean atmosphere. Visitors to Amsterdam experience a living, vital city which Amsterdammers are proud to share; in the words of Nicolas Freeling, creator of the famous Dutch detective, Van der Valk, 'I know of no city where the outsider is so spontaneously taken to heart'.

THOMAS COOK'S AMSTERDAM

Thomas Cook's first party to the Netherlands was organised in 1868. The following year he returned with a trip to the Amsterdam Exhibition. By 1899 Amsterdam was a regular feature of Cook's Tours. A brochure for that year advertised a conducted 'Easter tour to Holland and the Dead Cities of the Zuyder Zee', with first-class hotels and second-class travel, for £5 5s 0d. By then Thomas Cook had an office in Amsterdam, at 83 Damrak.

The 1911 brochure advertises carriages for a three-hour tour of the city, and a number of excursions including the island of Marken, Broek in Waterland ('the cleanest village in Holland' – which had no roads leading to it, for fear that horses would foul the streets), Edam and Zaandam, to see Peter the Great's cottage – still owned at the time by the Russian imperial family.

'From my favourite spot on the floor I look up at the blue sky and the bare chestnut tree on whose branches little raindrops glisten like silver, and at the seagulls and other birds as they glide on the wind.'
ANNE FRANK

'Heroic, Resolute, Compassionate.' The succinct motto on Amsterdam's coat of arms.

'What impressed contemporaries about Amsterdam was that it was a city entirely dedicated to making money . . . all the way up the Damrak the quay was crammed with hoists, piles of merchandise, porters and small ships loading and unloading . . . almost the whole world seemed to be assembled to buy and sell.'
MARK GIROUARD

'The pungent salt smell, the northern, maritime keynotes of seagull and herring, the pointed brick buildings, tall and narrow like herons, with their mosaic of particoloured shutters, eaves, sills that give the landscape their stiff, heraldic look . . .'
NICOLAS FREELING

'Amsterdam remains the refuge of all those striving to free themselves from the stifling atmosphere of small communities, and that too forms part of the city's strength and vitality.'
GEERT MAK

The canals of Amsterdam

The land

Amsterdam, meaning 'Amstelledamme', or 'dam across the River Amstel', is the commercial capital of the Netherlands though, unusually, the Dutch parliament is based in The Hague. Visitors incorrectly refer to the Netherlands as Holland, which is like saying England instead of Britain. Holland consists of only the two western provinces along the North Sea: Noord (North) Holland, where Amsterdam is located though Haarlem is the provincial capital, and Zuid (South) Holland, where The Hague is located, which is both the provincial capital and the seat of government.

Nord and Zuid Holland, along with the province of Utrecht (capital, Utrecht), form a region known as the *Randstad*, meaning 'ring town', so-called because its cities form an almost circular conurbation. It is also known, more affectionately, as 'the big village', and it has a population of over 4 million – 27 per cent of the Dutch total of 14.8 million.

The *Randstad* is economically prosperous, accounting for almost half the country's total output. Amsterdam itself is an important banking and financial services centre. Around a third of the city's income comes from small businesses and the self-employed. Despite its laid-back atmosphere, the city is a hive of enterprise, with many people employed in computer consultancy, graphic design, journalism, publishing, architecture and the arts. Tourism and retailing are also major sources of revenue and employment.

The other cities of the *Randstad* include Rotterdam, the world's biggest port, Delft, Leiden and Gouda. Schiphol airport is also critical to the *Randstad* economy. Most visitors see it only as an efficient passenger airport, but behind the scenes it has a huge freight-handling capacity and is a major distribution hub for European exports and imports – especially perishable goods, such as fruit, vegetables and cut flowers. Many of the exotic and out-of-season fruits that fill European supermarket shelves are flown into Schiphol from the Far East, Africa, the Caribbean and the Canary Islands for onward distribution by road.

This in turn has benefited the Dutch horticultural and agricultural industries. Much of the land to the south and west of Amsterdam is used for growing flowers, pot plants and greenhouse fruit and vegetables, such as tomatoes, peppers, cucumbers and strawberries. Tulip bulbs are the most famous product of the region, but in terms of sales they actually rank fourth behind roses, chrysanthemums and carnations. The bulb fields and gardens around Lisse, just south of Amsterdam, are a major tourist attraction in their own right, as is the world's largest daily flower auction at Aalsmeer, adjacent to Schiphol airport.

Much of the land around Amsterdam has been reclaimed over the centuries by constructing a complex system of dykes and dams to hold back the sea and drain the watery landscape. The resulting land is called polder, from *pol*, referring to the wooden poles or stakes that were originally used to stabilise the sides of the drainage dykes. Wind-powered mills were once used to raise the water through a series of ring canals, each one higher than the last, so that the water could eventually flow via natural rivers out to the sea. Nowadays the task of drainage is handled by electric pumps, but well-preserved windmills are still a characteristic feature of the Dutch landscape, especially to the north of Amsterdam, around Zaanse Schans.

The most recent area of polderisation lies immediately to the east of Amsterdam. The shallow IJsselmeer (formerly known as the Zuider Zee) was dammed in 1932 by building the 30km (19-mile) *Afsluitdijk* (Enclosing Dyke). Part of the IJsselmeer was then drained to create Flevoland; this huge area of reclaimed land, measuring 1,800sq km (695sq miles), was officially declared the 12th province of the Netherlands in 1986. Today such large-scale polderisation schemes are surrounded by controversy. Environmentalists fear that further drainage of the IJsselmeer would damage a fragile ecology. Furthermore, if the water table falls below its present level, the wooden piles supporting Amsterdam's older buildings might dry out and rot, causing damage on a massive scale. To the relief of Amsterdam residents, further schemes have been put on hold and a temporary truce has been drawn in the elemental battle between the land and the sea.

A land reclaimed from the sea

History

1275	First documented reference to the city.
1300	First municipal charter, the town now creates and enforces its own laws.
1323	The town prospers on trade with England, Germany and the Baltic.
1345	Pilgrims flock to Amsterdam after a communion host thrown into a fire is found intact in the embers and a miracle is declared.
1346	Begijnhof convent founded.
1452	New laws forbid the use of thatch and timber in favour of brick and tile after a devastating fire.
1519	Charles V of Spain inherits Amsterdam with the Habsburg Empire.
1535	Anabaptists riot in Amsterdam, sparking a Catholic backlash.
1566	Calvinists storm churches, winning the right to hold public services – an event known as the *Beeldenstorm*, the Iconoclasm.
1567	Philip II of Spain, heir to Charles V, imposes strict Catholic rule.
1572	The Dutch revolt against Spanish rule.
1578	Prince William's troops drive the Spanish from Amsterdam. Catholicism is outlawed and Calvinists take over city institutions, an event known as the *Alteratie*, the Alteration.
1579	Protestants from Antwerp come to Amsterdam, heralding the Golden Age.
1595–7	The Dutch discover sea routes to Indonesia.
1602	Dutch East India Company set up to co-ordinate Dutch Far East trade.
1613	Construction of the canal circle begins.
1621	The Dutch West India Company is set up to co-ordinate trade with the Americas and Africa.

1689 The Dutch prince, William III of Orange, is crowned King of England.

18th century Amsterdam's maritime trade is slowly crippled by a series of costly wars.

1795 The Velvet Revolution; French revolutionary troops are welcomed to Amsterdam by reformers who establish a new National Assembly.

1806 Napoleon sets his brother, Louis Napoleon, on the Dutch throne.

1813 The northern and southern provinces of the Netherlands are briefly united.

1831 The southern provinces form the Kingdom of Belgium.

1845 Riots lead to democratic reform and a directly elected parliament.

1848–76 The Noordzee Kanaal (North Sea Canal) and the discovery of new diamond fields in South Africa spell prosperity for Amsterdam.

1945 Amsterdam liberated from German occupation.

1963 Squatter protests against the housing problem.

1965 Anarchistic 'Provocateurs' win seats on the city council.

1975 Riots over plans to demolish an area of Nieuwmarkt to build the Metro system and Stadhuis complex.

1982 Rioting following the forcible eviction of squatters.

1994 Local council elections swing to the right.

1995 Increasing drug problems led to many coffeeshops being closed and the remainder licensed to sell cannabis only.

2002 Adoption of the euro. National election following the assassination Pim Fortuyn. The right-wing CDA-LPF coalition wins.

2005 Dutch voters reject a proposed EU constitution.

2007 A new public library opens in the eastern docklands area in July. Designed by Jo Coenen, it's Europe's largest.

2008 The city is named World Book Capital for its reputation as a refuge for free speech.

Politics

The Netherlands has a three-tier system of government: the national parliament based in Den Haag (The Hague) is responsible for defence, overall fiscal policy and foreign affairs; provincial councils based in each of the 12 provincial capitals are responsible for managing the local infrastructure; and city councils are responsible for running the large municipalities.

The system is highly devolved and the Amsterdam city council has a very wide range of powers and responsibilities, while national politics has very little impact on the city. In recent years the council has had to face an awesome range of issues, and it has developed progressive, though not always successful, policies to manage the problems of housing, unemployment, race relations, inner-city renewal, drugs and crime.

In the 1970s, what had hitherto been a series of relatively peaceful protests turned violent. On 'Blue Monday', 24 March 1975, police and protesters battled in the streets over plans to demolish an area of Nieuwmarkt to build the new Stadhuis or City Hall. In 1982, a state of emergency was declared after attempts by the police to evict squatters sparked off three days of rioting. Amsterdam was seen as one of the most troubled cities in Europe.

Today the anarchy of previous decades has given way to hard-headed pragmatism, tempered by traditional Dutch humanism. Local residents and shop owners have begun to form action groups to clean up their areas of the city and to apply pressure on the city council to tackle the problems of housing, drugs and petty crime.

Various experiments have been tried to tackle the drugs problem. Initially, non-Dutch addicts were deported and the remainder were given free heroin in an attempt to stamp out illegal dealing and petty crime. This proved unsuccessful and the authorities have now placed their hopes in a programme of medical help for heroin addicts, whose numbers have now stabilised.

On the housing front, the squatter movement had one lasting effect: the wholesale clearance of 'slum' areas has been halted in favour of sympathetic small-scale regeneration. The city owns 40 per cent of the housing stock and 70 per cent of the land; its policy now is to lease this to developers who build new apartments or restore old buildings for rent. Critics say that rents have soared as a result, and there are long waiting lists for attractive canal-side flats.

On the other hand, problems remain beyond the city centre. Amsterdam has a large ethnic community; nearly a third of the city's 743,000 population are of Turkish or Moroccan origin. Many were brought in as 'guest workers' in the 1960s; others originate from former Dutch colonies – the Antilles, Surinam and Indonesia. Many live in soulless tower blocks on estates such as Bijlmermeer, in the south of the city. Ironically, these flats, designed on the futuristic principles of Le Corbusier, were originally built as luxury apartments, but their intended occupants preferred to stay in the city centre.

Part of the answer has been to redevelop Bijlmermeer, replacing the tower blocks with new housing on a

Amsterdam's World Trade Centre

more human scale. Businesses have been encouraged to open up here as well as to provide much-needed local employment.

Amsterdam's problems have been made worse by the closure of several big industrial enterprises, such as the former shipyards. Other businesses have moved, many to Rotterdam. Heineken's decision to relocate to Zoeterwoude in 1986 was a further blow, even though residents had often complained about the smell of the brewery and its massive trucks clogging up the city's narrow roads.

In response to the threat of decline and unemployment, a huge regeneration scheme is under way in the redundant docklands area which stretches for 15km (9½ miles) behind Amsterdam Centraal Station. It is hoped that multinational companies will be attracted to set up corporate headquarters here from which to take advantage of the single European market.

In a complex city like Amsterdam it is difficult to find political solutions that please everyone, yet much has been achieved since the stormy days of the 1970s. Slowly but surely the city council is achieving its objective of *stadsvernieuwing* – urban renewal (the Zeedijk area, on the fringe of the red-light district, being the latest to benefit); instead of ending up a ghost town or a gigantic tourist theme park, Amsterdam remains an invigorating, cultural and energetic city that Amsterdammers genuinely like to live in.

Culture

Amsterdam has its own distinctive culture which embraces the extremes of tradition and the avant-garde. On the one hand, Amsterdammers are wedded to the old-world charm of brown cafés lit by schemerlampen, *twilight lamps that cast a golden glow. Crowds gather around streetside herring stalls in spring to sample the mild* nieuwe haring, *the first of the season, while all over the city bright ornate barrel organs pump out old-fashioned fairground music.*

On the other hand, this is a city that loves the experimental. Theatres mount productions in which the cast consists entirely of barking Alsatian dogs. Galleries host 'events' where participants transform each other into living works of art by daubing their naked bodies with paint. Amsterdam could never be accused of dreariness.

Such contradictions are part of the cultural diversity of a city which sometimes seems obsessed by art. Sometimes passions run out of control. *The Night Watch* has been attacked with knives and acid on some occasions by frustrated individuals, and years ago some masterpieces were taken from the Van Gogh Museum, but later turned in.

Such extreme gestures are hardly justified in a city that offers so many outlets for creative expression. Artists receive training grants and subsidies, and both public and commercial money is used to fund public murals, paintings or sculpture whenever a new building is erected in the city. Some of the city's buses and trams have been turned into mobile works of art by students of the Rietveld Academy. Even shopkeepers and homeowners enter into the spirit of artistic endeavour; the shopping streets of Jordaan and the canal circle are enlivened by eye-catching window displays, and the owners of smart canalside apartments leave their curtains open at night to reveal tasteful interiors – every item of furniture, every plant and picture carefully chosen to make a statement to any passer-by.

Several times a year Amsterdammers come together for big street festivals; for Queen's Day, Koninginnedag (30 April), for carnival, for the Aalsmeer to Amsterdam floral parade in the beginning of September and for the Jordaan festival in the middle of the month. Here again Amsterdam reveals its love of extremes. All heads turn at the arrival of a popular character, known simply as Fabiola, whose outlandish and inventive costumes have now become part of Amsterdam folklore. Further style is added by the ethnic costumes worn by the large number of Caribbean, Surinamese and Indonesian participants.

Other set-piece events attract festive crowds. In June some of the world's top performers come together for the three-week-long Holland Festival. On the last weekend in August, theatre, dance and music companies from all over the Netherlands perform extracts from the year's forthcoming programme in the streets of Amsterdam. This event, called the *Uitmarkt*, is a huge open-air arts market designed to sell advance tickets; for the visitor it provides an opportunity to sample the complete spectrum of the arts.

Every August (first weekend) the Gay Pride event is launched, with a canal parade throughout the city attracting 250,000 visitors who come to watch more than 80 wildly decorated boats occupied by extravagant celebrants in outrageous costumes. There are also cultural and sports events held all weekend.

From 19–23 August 2010, Amsterdam will be the home port for the eighth time to one of the largest maritime events in the world: Sail Amsterdam. Approximately 20 tall ships and 500 historic sailing boats and motor boats are expected at the IJ harbour in this international event.

Other events to look out for in the summer are the cheap and varying summer concerts in July and August in the famous Concertgebouw and the Grachten festival on Herengracht, Keizersgracht and Prinsengracht around the third Saturday of August. During the rest of the year the cultural calendar is packed with events: opera and ballet at the Muziektheater, concerts by the world-renowned Royal Concertgebouw Orchestra (under Mariss Jansons) or the Netherlands Philharmonic Orchestra, jazz at the Bimhuis, world music at the Melkweg (Milky Way), and rock concerts at Paradiso, not to mention scores of events hosted by small clubs and arts cafés. Amsterdam is famed for its tolerance and its live-and-let-live philosophy, and, in that atmosphere, cultural pluralism thrives – there is no taste, no matter how traditional or way-out, that is not catered for.

Celebrating Queen's Day on the river

Festivals

The people of Amsterdam are always ready to take to the streets and join in the spontaneous fun that surrounds their numerous festivals. Visitors are welcome to join in and flow with the crowd.

January

New Year is greeted with fireworks, a symbolic way of scaring off the devils of dreary winter. Revellers sustain themselves by consuming quantities of *oliebollen* (doughnuts) and champagne. The big squares see most of the action, and street performers entertain the crowds.

February/March

If the weather turns cold enough to freeze the canals and waterways, an event that occurs only once in every ten years or so, everyone brings out their skates. In the northern Netherlands (in Friesland), the big event is the **Elfstedentocht**, the 11-towns race, a real test of skaters' skill and stamina, which Amsterdammers keenly follow on television.

April

30 April is **Koninginnedag** (Queen's Day), the Queen's official birthday. Once this was a festival for children, who would set up stalls selling their handmade sweets and cakes or unwanted toys, to earn some pocket money, but today everyone joins in, setting up stalls in front of their homes so that Amsterdam turns into a huge street market. Street performers add to the fun and many bars set up outdoor stages where bands entertain the customers. Leidseplein and Vondelpark are the best places to savour the atmosphere.

May

After the **Commemoration of 4 May** for the victims of World War II, the end of the occupation is celebrated on the 5th as **Liberation Day**, with concerts, parties and processions.

June

The three-week-long **Holland Festival** is a prestigious showcase for the arts. Top performers from all over the world take part (programme information from Holland Festival, *Tel: (020) 523 7787; www.hollandfestival.nl*).

July

The **Over Het IJ Festival** is in full swing, with fringe-style arts events all over the north bank of the IJ river, reached by a (free) passenger ferry that goes from behind Centraal Station. Performances take place indoors and out, and range across the whole spectrum of progressive arts, from dance to electronic sound and light shows (*tel: (020) 492 2229* for information and bookings).

August

The Grachtenfestival, taking place from the second Wednesday to the second Saturday, provides free classical music on and around Prinsengracht, culminating in the concert on Saturday evening. This usually features a top international pianist who performs from a floating platform in front of the Pulitzer Hotel (Prinsengracht 315–331). Music-lovers come with picnics and champagne to line the canal banks (for information *tel: (020) 788 2000*).

At the end of the month there's the **Uitmarkt**, a huge cultural festival at which arts companies from all over the Netherlands perform, is held in its new location in the Eastern Harbour area.

September

The **Bloemen Corso** (Flower Parade), held on the first Saturday in September, is a spectacular affair organised by florists and horticulturalists; their huge, decorative floats are driven from the flower auction at Aalsmeer through the streets of Amsterdam to a reception in Dam Square, after which the parade is illuminated for the return.

The **Jordaan Festival**, in the third weekend of September, is a riotous fortnight of music, fancy dress and beer-drinking in which the Jordaan district extends a friendly welcome.

November/December

St Nicolaas, the Dutch equivalent of Santa Claus, arrives in Amsterdam on the second or third Saturday in November (around the 17th), arriving by steamboat 'from Spain' at Centraal Station and parading up Damrak, distributing sweets to crowds of children. Dutch children traditionally receive their presents on the **Feast of St Nicolaas** (5 December), although increasingly they are indulged with more presents on 25 December.

Singing the famous Jordaan song 'Geez mij maar Amsterdam' in celebration of Queen's Day

Impressions

The historic heart of Amsterdam is very compact and it can be crossed on foot in less than half an hour. Trams which depart from Amsterdam Centraal Station reach all parts of the city, and a Museumboat service circles the canal system every 30 minutes in summer from 9.30am–4.45pm.

Even so, the best way to get to know the city is to walk. If you take to the streets in comfortable shoes, you will be rewarded by glimpses of Amsterdam at work and play and discover the rich diversity of the city's architecture. Enticing shops selling flowers, crafts, antiques or books will arrest your attention, and when you are tired you can be sure there is a pavement café, serving coffee or *warme chocolade* (hot chocolate) topped with whipped cream, waiting just round the corner.

Another way to gain a swift overview of the city is to take a canal cruise; knowledgeable guides will point out the key buildings and features and, seen from the water as it was intended to be, Amsterdam takes on a whole new perspective.

AREA BY AREA

When viewed on a map, Amsterdam has a distinctive shape; its several districts lock together like pieces in a jigsaw, and they represent separate phases in the deliberately planned development of the city. Once you understand the city's layout you will find it easier to negotiate the cobweb-like pattern of canals, streets and squares.

The medieval city

Nearly everyone receives their first glimpse of Amsterdam from Centraal Station, the arrival point of trains from the airport and from all over Europe. The station stands on the site of the original harbour which was partly filled in during the 19th century. From Stationsplein, which is usually crowded with tourists and commuters, the city's main street – Damrak – leads to the main square. This is simply called Dam Square and, as the name suggests, it is built over the site of the original dam across the River Amstel, after which the city was named. This dam probably had lock gates, allowing small craft to pass through, and was designed to control the tidal flow of the river. Two of the city's most imposing buildings stand on the right-hand (western) side of the square: the Koninklijk Paleis (Royal Palace) and the Nieuwe Kerk (New Church).

Damrak runs through the heart of the oldest part of Amsterdam, dividing it into two parts which, on the map, look like a pair of lungs. To the east (left, with your back to the station) is the Oude Zijde (OZ), or Old Side, district, which was already built up by the 13th century. To the west is the slightly younger Nieuwe Zijde (NZ), or New Side, district, first developed in the 14th century.

Medieval Amsterdam was surrounded by a defensive rampart. This has since disappeared, but its position is indicated by the names of Oudezijds Voorburgwal and Oudezijds Achterburgwal, meaning, respectively,

in front of and behind the city wall. These two canals themselves started out as defensive moats. Their counterparts to the west, the Nieuwezijds Voorburgwal and Achterburgwal, have since been filled in.

The Canal Circle

Wrapped around the core of the medieval city is the Grachtengordel, the Canal Circle (or 'girdle'), consisting of three concentric canals built in the 17th century and the main focus of architectural interest in the city. The harbour end of the Canal Circle, around Brouwersgracht, was the first to be developed, beginning in 1613. As building progressed, the houses became ever grander; the point in the canal furthest from the harbour is known as the Golden Bend because of the wealth

The Royal Palace on Dam Square

Central Amsterdam

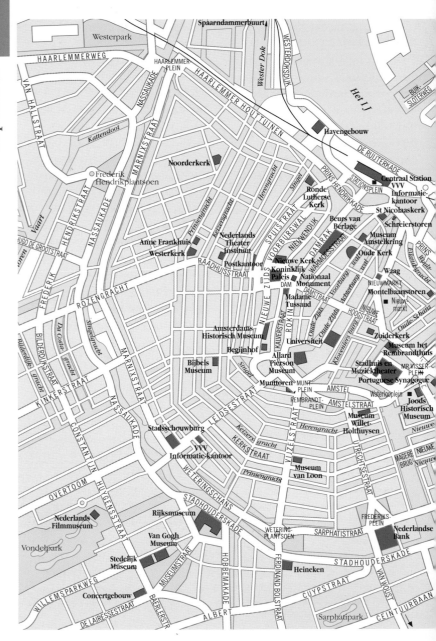

Westerpark

Spaarndammerbuurt

WESTERDOKSDIJK

Wester Dok

HAARLEMMERWEG

HAARLEMMER-
PLEIN

HAARLEMMER HOUTTUINEN

Het IJ

BUIK-
SLOTERWEG

Kattensloot

DE RUIJTERKADE

Hayengebouw

Noorderkerk

PRINS HENDRIKKADE

STATIONSPLEIN

Centraal Station
VVV
Informatie-
kantoor

Frederik
Hendrikplantsoen

Ronde
Lutherse
Kerk

SPUISTRAAT

VOORBURGWAL

NIEUWENDIJK

DAMRAK

Beurs van
Berlage

St Nicolaaskerk

Schreierstoren

Nederlands
Theater
Instituut

Museum
Amstelkring

Anne Frankhuis
Westerkerk

RAADHUISSTRAAT

Postkantoor

Nieuwe Kerk

WARMOESSTRAAT

Oude Kerk

Waag

HUGO DE GROOTSTRAAT

Koninklijk
Paleis

Nationaal
Monument

DAM

Voorburgwal

Achterburgwal

NIEUWMARKT

Montelbaanstoren

Madame
Tussaud

NIEUWE
ZIJDS

DAMSTRAAT

KALVERSTRAAT

ROKIN

Oude Zijds

Oude Zijds

NIEUWE
HOOGSTRAAT

Nieuw-
markt

ROZENGRACHT

MARNIXSTRAAT

Amsterdams
Historisch Museum

Universiteit

Kloveniers burg

Oude Schans

Zuiderkerk

Museum het
Rembrandthuis

Begijnhof

Allard
Pierson
Museum

Stadhuis en
Muziektheater

MR VISSER-
PLEIN

KINKERSTRAAT

Bijbels
Museum

Singel

Munttoren

MUNT-
PLEIN

AMSTEL

Portuguese Synagogue

Waterlooplein

Joods
Historisch
Museum

REMBRANDT-
PLEIN

AMSTELSTRAAT

Stadsschouwburg

LEIDSESTRAAT

Keizers gracht

VIJZELSTRAAT

Museum
Willet-
Holthuysen

Herengracht

Nieuwe

VVV
Informatie-kantoor

KERKSTRAAT

Prinsengracht

Museum
van Loon

UTRECHTSESTRAAT

MAGERE
BRUG

NIEUWE

OVERTOOM

HUYGENSSTRAAT

WETERINGSCHANS

STADHOUDERSKADE

WETERING-
PLANTSOEN

FREDERIKS-
PLEIN

SARPHATISTRAAT

Nederlands
Filmmuseum

Rijksmuseum

Nederlandse
Bank

Vondelpark

Van Gogh
Museum

MUSEUMSTRAAT

HOBBEMAKADE

FERDINAND BOLSTRAAT

STADHOUDERSKADE

VAN WOUST

Stedelijk
Museum

Heineken

WILLEMSPARKWEG

Concertgebouw

BAERLERSTR

DE LAIRESSESTRAAT

ALBERT

CUYPSTRAAT

Sarphatipark

CEINTUURBAAN

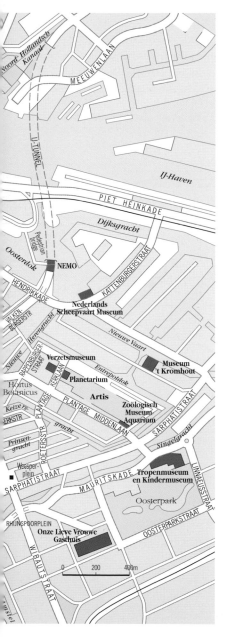

of its former inhabitants and the palatial splendour of their houses, many of which now serve as bank premises and estate agencies.

The Museum Quarter

Not far from the Golden Bend is the Museum Kwartier (Museum Quarter), a wedge-shaped block built as an extension to the city in the 19th century. Here you will find the famous Rijksmuseum and Van Gogh Museum, as well as the Stedelijk Museum of Modern Art set to reopen in 2009 (visit *www.stedelijk.nl* for the latest information). Bordering the Museum Quarter are Vondelpark, the scene of open-air concerts in summer, and the Concertgebouw, famed for its orchestra and excellent acoustics.

A short way further out is the district called De Pijp (The Pipe), because of its long, narrow tunnel-like streets. The principal thoroughfare, Albert Cuypstraat, hosts a bustling and colourful street market where it is possible to buy just about anything. The street is also renowned for its inexpensive ethnic restaurants and the Van Moppes Diamonds factory.

The Museum Quarter is linked to the city centre by Nieuwe Spiegelstraat, which ends close to the Golden Bend. It has the biggest concentration of antique shops in Amsterdam and makes for fascinating browsing. The canal circle continues round from here until it is interrupted by the River Amstel. It then continues for a short way on the opposite bank to meet the district known as Plantage. As the name suggests, this is a leafy suburb which was originally laid out as a pleasure garden; by the late 18th century wealthy businessmen began to build country houses here, but several large green spaces remain, such as the zoo (known as Natura Artis Magistra, or just Artis) and the Hortus Botanicus Plantage (Botanical Gardens).

The Jewish Quarter

Coming back towards the city centre, the next district is Jodenbuurt, the former Jewish Quarter, with its synagogue, the Jewish Historical Museum and the Museum Het Rembrandthuis (Rembrandt's House). Jodenbuurt has been comprehensively redeveloped since World War II and has a character entirely different to the rest of central Amsterdam, dominated as it is by the controversial new Stadhuis (City Hall) and the Muziektheater complex, home to the Netherlands Opera and National Ballet.

The familiar Amsterdam of characterful canals and old houses returns as you cross from Jodenbuurt into Nieuwmarkt, a district of great contrasts. To the south is the attractive maze of buildings forming the university, while to the north, around Zeedijk, are the red-light district and Chinatown.

Amsterdam has several other districts of note. The eastern harbour, adjacent to Plantage and Jodenbuurt, has numerous old warehouses recently converted to

apartments, and the interesting NEMO science and technology museum. On the other side of the city, Jordaan (from the French *jardin*, garden) was, despite its name, an industrial suburb of narrow lanes and cramped workshops. Today it is a characterful neighbourhood of

Greater Amsterdam

craft and speciality shops and ethnic restaurants.

The character of Amsterdam

Amsterdam is an overgrown village, a comfortable, congenial city whose relaxed pace is symbolised by the lumbering old-fashioned bicycles adopted by many residents for getting about, or the barges that make their sedate progress along the city's numerous canals.

At the same time, there are aspects to the city that may puzzle or shock the

first-time visitor. Ugly graffiti disfigures many fine buildings and some streets are still slippery with dog faeces. Dishevelled drug addicts loiter around the city, 'smoking bars' openly serve marijuana-laced cigarettes or cakes, and prostitutes operate in full public view from sitting rooms lit by red neon.

This side of Amsterdam reflects the city's live-and-let-live attitude, a philosophical outlook whose pluses and minuses are a frequent topic of debate among Amsterdammers themselves. Fundamentally, Amsterdammers value

freedom from interference – whether from neighbours or officialdom. In their respect for privacy they turn a blind eye to what others choose to do, but are less tolerant of the antisocial behaviour of dog owners and rebellious adolescents with spray cans.

As a result, Amsterdam has a permissive culture, but one that has been exploited by the unscrupulous few, including the many drug dealers and pornographers who have tarnished the city's image. Though the municipality takes action against

The Magere Brug or 'Skinny Bridge'

The Jewish Historical Museum is devoted to the history of Amsterdam's Jewish population

impudent behaviour, this still casts a shadow over what local people consider real achievements, such as racial harmony, the espousal of gay rights and sexual equality.

Amsterdammers will talk about such issues with humour and frankness; one of the delights of the city is the ease with which people engage in conversation, even with total strangers. They have the linguistic skills to do so; 70 per cent of the city's population speaks English and many also speak French and German. The Dutch

BICYCLES

The bicycle is Amsterdam's favourite mode of transport – there are 550,000 bikes in a city of 735,000 people, many of them painted with colourful designs and transformed into minor works of art. The White Bikes scheme of 1966 was intended to provide free cycles for everyone; the scheme foundered in days when all the bikes were stolen, repainted and sold.

educational system encourages language learning from an early age and Amsterdammers remain linguistically adroit by watching or listening to European TV and radio; many prefer

Just one of many second-hand bookstores

the output of the British BBC to that of their own rather stolid national broadcasting authority.

They also read voraciously – Amsterdam is one of Europe's largest markets for books, and shelves full of well-thumbed volumes in several languages are an essential part of the furnishings in any self-respecting city home. Central to all this is one overriding characteristic: respect for the quality of life. Amsterdammers are entrepreneurial but not workaholic; furthering their careers is less important than family life, time

PLACE NAMES

To find your way about Amsterdam it helps to know that *plein* means square, *straat* street, *kerk* church, *huis* house and *gracht* canal. The three main canals are Herengracht (the Gentlemen's Canal), Keizersgracht (the Emperor's Canal, named after the Holy Roman Emperor, Maximilian I), and Prinsengracht (Prince's Canal, named after Prince William of Orange who liberated the city from Spanish rule).

spent with friends, or a visit to the theatre. Many visitors find that this refreshing and admirable attitude is highly infectious.

Lido Casino on Singelgracht

Amsterdam

'*Where else in the world could one choose a place where all life's commodities and all the curiosities one could wish for are so easy to find as here?*'

RENÉ DESCARTES

Agnietenkapel

The Agnietenkapel is a simple but graceful chapel dating from 1470 and once part of the convent of St Agnes. In 1632 it was taken over by the Atheneum Illustre, a learned body out of which the University of Amsterdam was later to evolve. Part of the chapel was converted into a lecture theatre, the Grote Gehoorzaal, which has a fine wooden ceiling decorated with Renaissance motifs and a portrait of Minerva, goddess of wisdom. The walls of the theatre are hung with 17th-century portraits of illustrious and learned figures of the age. The rest of the building is used for university events, which means admission has become limited to outside visitors. The Universiteitsmuseum (University Museum), a collection covering the history of education and student life in the city, has relocated to *Oude Turfmarkt 129. Tel: (020) 525 2473. Open: Mon–Fri 10am–5pm, Sat–Sun and holidays 1–5pm.*

Oudezijds Voorburgwal 231. Tel: (020) 525 9111. Tram: 4, 9, 14, 16, 24 or 25. Nearby: Allard Pierson Museum.

Allard Pierson Museum

This little-visited museum houses the University of Amsterdam's rich collection of archaeological material – mainly from ancient Egypt, Greece, Rome, Tuscany and the Near East. It also displays plaster casts of ancient Greek and Roman sculpture and occasionally mounts excellent special exhibitions on specific themes. *Oude Turfmarkt 127. Tel: (020) 525 2556; www.uba.uva.nl/apm. Open: Tue–Fri 10am–5pm, weekends & public holidays 1–5pm. Closed: Mon, 1 Jan, Easter Sunday, 30 Apr, Whit Sunday, 25 & 31 Dec. Admission charge. Tram: 4, 9, 16, 24 or 25. Nearby: Agnietenkapel, the University Quarter (see pp96–7).*

Amstelkring Museum

The Amstelkring Museum is also known as *Ons Lieve Heer op Solder*

(Our Lord in the Attic) because, concealed in the roof space of this group of three houses, there is a clandestine Catholic church. The delightful museum thus provides two quite different experiences. At one level, this is a fine example of a wealthy merchant's residence, built by Jan Hartman in 1661, complete with contemporary furnishings. But one sober-looking cupboard opens up to reveal bawdy, low-life scenes painted on the insides of the door! Upstairs is a splendid Baroque church with ingenious foldaway pulpit and altar, and hiding places for the priest and communion plate. Clandestine churches such as this date from the *Alteratie*, the Alteration of 1578. Until then Amsterdam was a Catholic city, but tolerant of Protestants and free-thinkers, refugees from persecution in other parts of Europe. Calvinists formed a large and influential group, but they were forbidden from holding public services until they rioted in 1568, breaking into the city's churches and smashing statues, an event known as the *Beeldenstorm*, the Iconoclasm.

Order was restored when Calvinists were given their own church in the city, but this in turn provoked a reaction from that staunch defender of the Catholic faith, Philip II of Spain. He sent 10,000 troops under the Duke of Alva, Fernando Alvarez de Toledo, to restore strict Catholic order in the Netherlands. Many Calvinists in Amsterdam were executed and others fled to England.

The Dutch revolt against Spanish repression began in 1572 under the leadership of William the Silent, Prince of Orange, whose volunteer army slowly drove the Spanish southwards, to the area of modern Belgium. They liberated Amsterdam in 1578, the year of the *Alteratie*, so-called because Protestants took over all the city's institutions, and Catholicism, from then onwards, was banned – hence the growth of secret churches, of which the Amstelkring Museum has the best-preserved example.

In 1661, when this church was built, Catholics still went to great lengths to conceal their worship. By 1740, when the church was remodelled and given its galleries, capable of seating 200 people, it could scarcely still be operating without the knowledge of the authorities, who must simply have turned a blind eye. The ban on Catholicism was finally lifted in the 19th century when the nearby church of Sint Nicolaas was built, now standing forlorn and rarely used on the harbour, opposite Amsterdam Centraal Station.

Oudezijds Voorburgwal 40. Tel: (020) 624 6604; www.museumamstelkring.nl. Open: Mon–Sat 10am–5pm, Sun & public holidays 1–5pm. Closed: 1 Jan & 30 Apr. On 31 Dec the museum shuts at 4pm. Admission charge. Tram: 4, 9, 16, 24 & 25. Nearby: Oude Kerk (see p47).

The Grachtengordel

Amsterdam's remarkable Grachtengordel, or Canal Ring, represents one of the earliest examples of deliberate town planning in Europe. The scheme was devised by Hendrik Staets, the municipal carpenter, in 1609. His plan for the controlled expansion of the city has an elegant logic. Three new canals were dug, the Herengracht, Keizersgracht and Prinsengracht, with a combined length of 12km (7 miles). Each canal is 25m (82ft) wide, broad enough to accommodate four lanes of barges or lighters, the small, shallow-draughted boats used to unload cargo from bigger ships moored in the harbour. Up to 4,000 boats could be accommodated and 17th-century engravings show the canal circle as a forest of masts, its wide, tree-shaded quays bustling with porters.

Housing plots were sold to merchants with precisely 30m (98ft) of frontage, though some variation can be detected among the general uniformity; sometimes property

The view from the Oude Kerk, showing variations on a theme of pantiles and Flemish roofs

Though there have been some modern and inelegant encroachments, the roofscape of Amsterdam remains remarkably intact and unspoiled

speculators bought up two adjoining plots and resold them as one, enabling palatial residences to be built, or they subdivided them into three narrower plots.

Planning laws stipulated the maximum depth of houses to ensure a degree of space and light between houses backing on to each other on adjacent canals. This garden space was, in some cases, built over at a later date to provide an *achterhuis*, a back annexe, such as the one in which Anne Frank and her family hid from Nazi persecution. Even so, the canal circle still has numerous hidden gardens, as anyone who climbs the tower of Westerkerk will discover.

Shops were only permitted on the narrow interlinking radial canals, which is where they are still found to this day. This policy ensured that the three principal canals present an unbroken vista of houses, individualised by ornate gables and cornices, sculptural reliefs and fine doorcases; spotting the endless variations is one of the great pleasures of a leisurely stroll round this most elegant of cities.

Walk: Central Amsterdam

Starting at Amsterdam Centraal Station, this walk covers the main sights of the city centre and is intended to help you gain your bearings.

Allow 1 hour.

1 Amsterdam Centraal

Amsterdam's palatial railway station was built in 1889 by PJH Cuypers, the same architect who designed the Rijksmuseum. In its time the station was so admired that the Japanese built Tokyo station in the same style.
With your back to the station look over to the left.

2 VVV Informatiekantoor (Tourist Information)

The city's main tourist information office is located on the upper floor of a pretty timber building; below is the Noord-Zuid Hollandsch Koffiehuis (Coffee House), a popular spot for cakes and coffee.
Walk across Stationsplein and up Damrak.

3 Damrak

On the left, a duck pond is all that remains of Amsterdam's original harbour. Further up, the Beurs van Berlage stands on the site of the original Amsterdam Exchange. It was rebuilt in late 19th-century style from 1896 to 1903 by HP Berlage and recently converted for use as a cultural centre. Next comes De Bijenkorf (The Beehive), which is the city's biggest department store.
Continue up Damrak to Dam Square.

4 Dam Square

To the right of the city's main square is the former Stadhuis (Town Hall), renamed the Koninklijk Paleis (Royal Palace) when Louis Napoleon took up residence in 1808. It is partnered by the tall Gothic Nieuwe Kerk (New Church) which was begun in 1408.

To the left is the Nationaal Monument commemorating the dead of World War II. The obelisk contains urns of earth from each Dutch province and from Indonesia. The inscription reads 'Never again'.
Cross the square to the right of the Peek & Cloppenburg department store and enter Kalverstraat, one of the city's main

shopping streets. Halfway down, look for a lopsided gateway dated 1581.

5 Amsterdams Historisch Museum

The gate leads to the former municipal orphanage, now the Historical Museum. Walk into the arcaded courtyard and left, through glass doors, into the Civic Guard Gallery; this corridor is lined with 17th-century portraits of the city's militia units. *At the opposite end of the gallery, exit, turn right and, keeping left, descend two steps into the Begijnhof.*

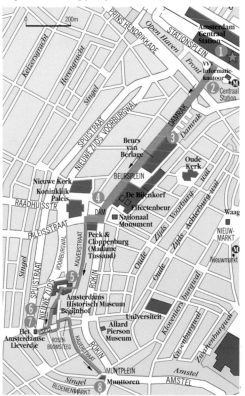

6 Begijnhof

This former convent is now a home for *ongehuwde dames* (unmarried ladies). Follow the path to the Engelsekerk (English Church), built in 1607. Opposite is Het Houten Huis (The Wooden House), built in 1460 and the oldest surviving building in Amsterdam. *Alongside is a passage leading out on to Spui. Turn right and cross to the paved area in front of the Athenaeum Bookshop.*

7 Het Amsterdamse Lieverdje

The name of this bronze statue means 'The Lovable Rascal of Amsterdam' and it is surrounded by bookshops, popular pavement cafés and a book market every Friday. *Retrace your steps past the Begijnhof entrance and walk down Rozenboomsteeg, past the elegant Empire-style building that houses Esprit. Turn right in Kalverstraat and continue all the way to the Munttoren.*

8 Munttoren

This grey stone tower was once a gate in the medieval city wall. The carillon of bells plays every 15 minutes. The walk ends just across the bridge to the right of the tower – at the Bloemenmarkt, where traders sell flowers and plants from floating barges. *To return to Dam Square, simply retrace your steps down Kalverstraat.*

Amsterdams Historisch Museum

The Amsterdam Historical Museum is a must for those who want to understand the history and development of the city. It is located just off Kalverstraat, the city's main shopping thoroughfare. The entrance is easy to miss – just a narrow leaning gateway decorated with the imperial crown and triple cross of Amsterdam's coat of arms. Below, a sculptural relief of children dressed in blue and red uniforms reminds us that the museum occupies the buildings of the former municipal orphanage, founded in 1580 on the site of St Lucien's convent. When you pass through the arch, the museum café is on the right, occupying the former convent dairy. It serves excellent pancakes and is known as 'David and Goliath Café' after the huge wooden fairground figures of David and Goliath standing at one end.

The Golden Age relived in the Historical Museum

Beyond lies a series of beautifully restored buildings designed by two leading 17th-century architects, Hendrik de Keyser and Jacob van Campen. They surround quiet cobbled courtyards where the orphanage children used to play. The prestige of the buildings is an indication of the city's enlightened policy in providing for the care of the poor – long before the idea of a welfare state was conceived.

It is a good idea to start your visit to the museum in room 1 (on the ground floor) where you can experience a newly installed multimedia presentation that will acquaint you with the museum collection.

The next two rooms (2 and 3) contain archaeological finds, reconstructed rooms and contemporary paintings illustrating life and industry in the medieval city. A part of room 3, for instance, is devoted to the Miracle of Amsterdam which occurred in 1345. The rather unsavoury details concern a dying man who was given communion as part of the Last Rites but who vomited up the host; this was thrown on a fire but found intact in the embers the next day. A miracle was declared and Amsterdam became a pilgrimage centre, so important that even the Holy Roman Emperor, Maximilian I, came to be cured of an illness. The Miracle is still celebrated today by up to 10,000 Catholics who take part in the *Stille Omgang* – the Silent Procession – which passes through the city's streets the second Sunday in March.

Room 4 houses the famous woodcut of 1544 by Cornelis Anthoniszoon, showing a three-dimensional bird's-eye view of the city and its bustling harbour. Clearly visible on this map is the original dam across the Amstel and its associated sea dyke walls.

Rooms 4 to 7 illustrate aspects of the city in the 16th century and especially the Golden Age (17th century). Another illuminated map shows the main Dutch voyages of discovery that set out from Amsterdam from 1595 looking first for a northeastern passage to the East Indies, then blazing a trail round the Cape of Good Hope. Typical eastern imports are displayed – blue-and-white Chinese porcelain that gave rise to the Dutch Delftware industry, sugar, tea and spices. A colourful contemporary painting shows Dam Square at that time, crowded with beggars, street musicians, artists selling their products, prosperous burghers in their finery – in fact little different from today, except for the changes in dress!

Rooms 8 to 11 (on the first floor) look at the art and crafts of the 17th century, and a small loft above Room 10 is devoted to carillon music, a distinctive feature of the city's churches; here you can sit at a keyboard and play tunes on bells suspended above.

Before you go to room 11 you could visit the Civic Guard Gallery, a glassed-in public thoroughfare hung with militia company portraits. Room 11 itself contains more group portraits – of the regents who supervised the city's

Arms and armour on display

charitable institutions, including Rembrandt's painting, *The Anatomy Lesson of Dr Deijman*.

Room 12 gives an insight into bourgeois life in 18th-century Amsterdam, all ponderous furniture and silverware, before livening up again with a brief account of industry. The museum concludes (in rooms 13 to 21 on the first floor and rooms 22 to 24 on the second floor) with the recent history of Amsterdam, from 1815 to the present. A pick of topics: social relations in the 19th century; fashion 'palaces'; World War II; the Sixties, stamped by the anti-establishment Provo movement; gay rights; the letters of Anne Frank.

Entrances at Kalverstraat 92.
Tel: (020) 523 1822; www.ahm.nl.
Open: weekdays 10am–5pm, weekends & public holidays 11am–5pm.
Closed: 1 Jan, 30 Apr & 25 Dec.
Admission charge. Tram: 1, 2, 4, 5, 9, 16, 24 & 25. Nearby: Begijnhof (see p38).

Anne Frankhuis

The Anne Frank House attracts more then half a million visitors a year and in summer it is essential to go early in the day to avoid long queues and crowded rooms. Alternatively, the museum tends to be quieter in the evening, and as it is open until 9pm, you may wish to delay your visit until later to avoid queues.

The house is tucked away on quiet Prinsengracht in the shadow of Westerkerk's tower, whose bells are lyrically described in Anne Frank's famous diary. It is a typical merchant's house, built in 1635, with an *achterhuis*, or back extension, added in 1740. In this attic the Frank family hid from July 1942 to August 1944.

The Franks had already escaped from Nazi persecution once in their lives; in 1933 they left their native Frankfurt, where Anne was born in 1929, and moved to Amsterdam, where they lived happily enough for seven years.

On 14 May 1940, the Nazis bombed Rotterdam: 800 people, mostly innocent civilians, were killed, 24,000 homes were destroyed and 50,000 people were left homeless. The Germans warned that they would next bomb Den Haag (The Hague), then Utrecht and all other Dutch cities in turn. Faced with such appalling aggression the Dutch had no choice but to surrender on 15 May: that night, knowing what was to come, 150 Jews in Amsterdam committed suicide.

Anti-Jewish measures began in earnest in 1940 with a series of prohibitive proclamations: Jews could not enter public places – swimming pools, parks and cinemas – or use public transport; all Jewish businesses had to be registered.

In February 1941, the Jewish Quarter of the city was closed off and the first of a series of round-ups, *razzias*, began. Thousands were arrested, herded into trains and sent off to Westerbork, a concentration camp on the Dutch–German border.

In 1942, Anne Frank's father, Otto, decided that the best course of action was to 'dive' – *onderduiken* – simply to disappear. He prepared a hiding place in the house that served as his company's office and warehouse. On 5 July a deportation order arrived, calling up Otto's eldest daughter, Margot, for 'work' at Westerbork. The next morning the family disappeared into the attic of Prinsengracht 263, their hiding place protected by nothing more solid than a bookcase concealing the stairs to the back of the house.

Inside the haunting Anne Frank House

The back extension of this typical merchant's house hid the Frank family for two years

of the secret household, only Otto Frank survived.

The Anne Frank House remains as it was in 1944, bare of furniture, which was looted after the family was deported. There are magazine pictures of film stars pasted on the wall by Anne and pencil marks recording the heights of the two growing sisters. The exhibitions mounted by the Anne Frank House are dedicated to combating prejudice, racism and discrimination in all its forms. In 1999, a building next door was taken over and renovated for extra exhibition and educational facilities, as well as a café and gift shop.

Anne Frank's diary, *Het Achterhuis* ('The Annexe'), was found lying on the floor after the family was arrested. It has since been published in 51 languages and vividly records the daily routine of life in the secret annexe, as well as the growing maturity of a naturally gifted writer, doomed to a tragic end.

The Franks were joined by the van Daan family and a dentist, Albert Dussel. For two years this clandestine household survived with the help of Otto Frank's Dutch partners and his two office girls, Miep and Elli. Food was provided by a local greengrocer, one of several who played their part in the Resistance by supplying 'divers'.

Not everyone was so altruistic. Someone – never identified – betrayed the Franks to the Nazis in 1944. They were arrested and sent to Westerbork, by then a staging post for Bergen-Belsen, where Anne Frank died of hunger and disease in March 1945, aged 15. Of all the eight members

One of the last entries in the diary states: 'I want to live on after my death'. That wish, at least, has been achieved. *Prinsengracht 267 (entree). Tel: (020) 556 7105; www.annefrank.org. Open: daily 15 Mar–14 Sept 9am–9pm (except 4 May & 26 June 9am–7pm); 15 Sept–14 Mar 9am–7pm (except 1 Jan noon–7pm, 20 Dec 9am–5pm, 25 Dec noon–5pm, 31 Dec 9am–5pm). Closed: Yom Kippur. Admission charge. Tram: 13, 14 & 17. Bus: 21, 170, 171 & 172. Nearby: Westerkerk (see p48).*

Walk: Around Brouwersgracht

This walk covers the oldest part of the canal circle, the harbour end, which was laid out from 1613.

Allow 1½ hours.

Start at Amsterdam Centraal Station. Walk up Damrak, take the first alley on the right, Haringpakkerssteeg, then bear right in Nieuwendijk. Cross busy Martelaarsgracht, turn left up Spuistraat and take the first right, Kattengat.

1 Ronde Lutherse Kerk

The big building on the left, with its green copper dome, is the Lutheran Round Church, built in 1668. Beside the church are two attractive step-gabled houses built in 1614 by Hendrik de Keyser.

Walk on past the Round Church, into Stromarkt (Straw Market), then left on to Singel.

2 Singel

Number 7 is the smallest house in Amsterdam, only a door's width wide. The builder may have done this to avoid property taxes, which were levied according to the façade width. To the right is Haarlemmersluis (Haarlem Lock); before the IJsselmeer was

dammed, this lock controlled the canal network water level.

Walk back up Singel, cross the bridge by the lock, turn left down the opposite bank of Singel and right into Brouwersgracht.

3 Brouwersgracht

The right bank of the Brewers' Canal is lined with attractively converted 17th-century warehouses while the canal itself is crossed by numerous bridges.

Continue along Brouwersgracht to the Prinsengracht junction and turn left up to Noorderkerk.

4 Noorderkerk (North Church)

This vast church was built in 1620 to serve the working-class district of Jordaan. The square in front hosts the Boerenmarkt (Farmers' Market) on Saturdays, the Lapjesmarkt, a large flea market (mainly for clothes), on Mondays.

Cross the next bridge left and walk down the opposite bank of Prinsengracht. Church concerts on Sat 2pm.

5 Hofjes

Two *hofjes*, or almshouses, can be visited. Zon's Hofje (Nos 159–171; push the door open and walk down the corridor) is a tree-shaded courtyard dating from 1765. Van Brienenhofje (Nos 89–133) dates from 1804 – legend has it that Jan van Brienen, a merchant, founded it after he was rescued, having locked himself inside his own safe.
Backtrack up Prinsengracht and turn left to explore Prinsenstraat and Herenstraat, then walk up Keizersgracht.

6 Het Huis met de Hoofden

The 'House with the Heads', Keizersgracht 123, was built by Hendrik de Keyser in 1623 and is decorated with busts of Greek deities.
Turn right on Leliegracht, a street noted for its bookshops, especially No 22, Architectura et Natura. Turn left on Prinsengracht.

7 Anne Frankhuis

Prinsengracht 263 is where Anne Frank wrote her famous diary while hiding with her family from the Nazis.
Continue a short way up to Westerkerk.

8 Westerkerk

The West Church (*see p48*) was built to Hendrik de Keyser's design in 1623 and its tower can be climbed for a bird's-eye view of the canal circle. They say that Rembrandt may be buried here.
From Westerkerk, turn left and follow Raadhuisstraat to return to Dam Square.

NEARBY

Walking down Raadhuisstraat, take a diversion to the left a short way into Herengracht for the ornate Bartolotti House (Nos 170–172), and the Theatermuseum next door (No 168).

Walk: Around Brouwersgracht

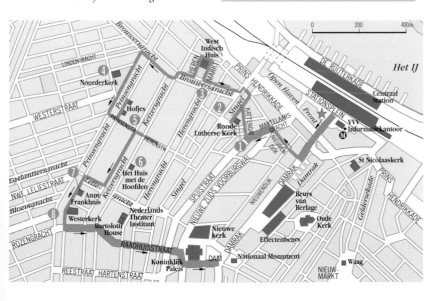

Artis Royal Zoo Amsterdam (Natura Artis Magistra)

Amsterdam's zoo opened in 1838 under the grand title of Natura Artis Magistra (Nature, Teacher of the Arts). Now known simply as Artis, the zoo offers enough attractions to fill the best part of a day. As well as 6,000 animals kept in naturalistic enclosures, there is a children's farm, a spectacular planetarium, a tropical house and a large aquarium. The ticket includes admission to two museums on the site – the Geologisch Museum illustrating the earth's evolution and the Zoologisch Museum whose tableaux and audio-visuals explain the flora and fauna of characteristic Dutch landscapes.

Plantage Kerklaan 40. Tel: (020) 523 3400; www.artis.nl. Open: daily 9am–5pm, Apr–Sept until 6pm. Planetarium: closed Mon until 12.30pm. Zoologisch Museum: same hours as Artis. Admission charge. Tram: 6, 9 & 14. Nearby: Hortus Botanicus Plantage.

Animal antics at the zoo

Begijnhof

The Begijnhof is a secluded oasis of peace in the bustling heart of the city. The entrance, easily missed, is a narrow door on Spui that leads into a flowery tree-shaded courtyard where neat gardens front some of Amsterdam's most charming houses. Number 34, known as **Het Houten Huis** or Wooden House, is the oldest surviving in the city, dating back to around 1470.

The Begijnhof was founded in 1346 as a convent for Beguines, named after Lambert de Begué who founded the order in Liège in the 12th century. The order – popular in the Low Countries and Germany – enabled women to live in a convent, devoting themselves to charitable work, but without taking vows of poverty, obedience and chastity. They remained free to own property, leave the convent and marry.

After the *Alteratie* of 1578 (*see* Amstelkring Museum, *pp26–7*) when Catholic institutions were taken over by Protestants, the Beguines were allowed to continue their work of education, caring for the poor and nursing the sick. They could worship only in secret, however, and a clandestine chapel, the Begijnhofkapel, was built in 1671, hidden behind the domestic façade of No 30. The chapel can be visited; its entrance is opposite the former convent church, handed over to Scottish Presbyterians in 1607 and subsequently renamed the Engelse Kerk, the English Church. This was rebuilt in 1727, and a more recent addition is the pulpit, with panels designed by Mondrian. As well as remaining the main church of Amsterdam's British community, the Engelse Kerk (English Reformed Church) hosts a series of free afternoon concerts from April–October and evening concerts during the rest of the year (details posted at the church door, or telephone *(020) 624 9665)*.

Many of the buildings of the Begijnhof were 'modernised' by the addition of new façades in the 17th and 18th centuries. The last of the Beguines died in 1971 and the houses are now let, for a nominal rent, to elderly women.

Entrance at Spui No 14 or from the Amsterdam Historical Museum.
Open: daily 9am–5pm.
Begijnhofkapel open daily 9am–5pm;
www.begijnhofamsterdam.nl.
Engelse Kerk open: only for concerts and for services on Sun at 10.30am. Free admission. Tram: 1, 2, 4, 5, 9, 16, 24 & 25. Nearby: Amsterdams Historich Museum (see pp32–3).

Beurs van Berlage

Amsterdam's Beurs, the former Stock Exchange, was reopened as a cultural centre in 1988, and is worth visiting for its interesting exhibitions and for concerts given by the Netherlands Philharmonic and Chamber Orchestras who have their home here, and as an architectural spectacle in its own right. The Beurs was rebuilt from 1896 to 1903 by Hendrick Petrus Berlage, the best Dutch architect of his age, in an imaginative style that anticipates the work of the early 1900s' Amsterdam School and is regarded as the Netherland's most important 20th-century building. The superb interiors are a tour de force of patterned brickwork and colourful tiles under a glass and wrought-iron roof. The building is used for changing exhibitions, and is only open during these.
Damrak 277. Tel: (020) 530 4141 (general enquiries); (020) 521 7520 (box office); www.beursvanberlage.nl. Box office open: Tue–Fri 2–5pm, other times for concerts. Tram: 4, 9, 16, 24 & 25. The Beurs is best seen by visiting an exhibition or joining a guided architectural tour. Nearby: Oude Kerk (see p47).

The impressive interior of the Biblical Museum showcases the design of leading Golden Age architect Philip Vingaboons

Canal life

Canals give Amsterdam its distinctive character, but it is a mistake to call the city the 'Venice of the North'. Amsterdammers are proud that their city is a vital, living place – to them Venice is a dead city, a theme park abandoned to tourism.

Swans, ducks and fish have made a very welcome return to the canals following a 15-year clean-up campaign. Dredgers keep the canal bottoms clear of debris – everything from abandoned bicycles to the cars of careless drivers who ended up in the water.

Until the IJsselmeer was dammed, the canals were flushed twice daily by natural tidal flow. Now a complex system of sluices and mechanical pumps does the job instead. Every night a third of the water in the canals is replaced by fresh water from the IJsselmeer. Excess water can also be pumped out if flood waters threaten the city after a period of heavy rain.

Nearly 5,000 people call the canals home

Today the canals are quiet backwaters where people can relax on their houseboats, take strolls and simply stare into the water

There are 160 separate canals in the city totalling 75km (47 miles) in length – spanned by 1,281 bridges, many of which are illuminated at night. Most of the bridges are fixed but several old wooden drawbridges remain, like the Magere Brug across the Amstel, topped by huge wooden balance beams that enable the central portion to be raised to admit tall-masted boats.

Nearly 5,000 people in Amsterdam live in 2,400 boats. These range from lovingly restored barges, gaily painted and bright with rooftop gardens, to utilitarian floating sheds. Living on a canal boat is not a cheap option; the cost of a boat and mooring is about the same as the rent for an equivalent-sized flat, but for boat dwellers it is a deliberately chosen way of life. Some Amsterdammers consider the canals a wasted asset since little use is made of their transport potential. Perhaps this situation will change if the city ever gets round to banning the automobile.

Walk: The Old Side

This walk covers the oldest part of the city, the Oude Zijde (Old Side) district, often simply abbreviated to OZ. The area is also known to locals as Wallen (Walls), because the two main canals – OZ Voorburgwal and OZ Achterburgwal – once lay on either side of the medieval ramparts.

Allow 2 hours.

Start on Dam Square and walk across to the Grand Hotel Krasnapolsky, turning left down Warmoesstraat.

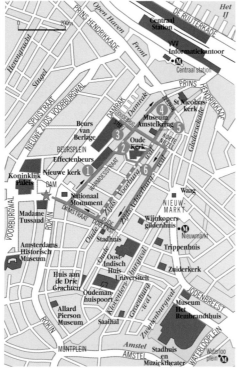

1 Warmoesstraat

Number 141 is the Condomerie Het Gulden Vlies (Golden Fleece), selling nothing but gift-wrapped condoms. Next door is an art gallery selling work by the council tenants who live above. Opposite is the **Effectenbeurs**, the modern Stock Exchange. Further down is the elegant Thee en Koffiehandel, an old-fashioned tea and coffee merchant. *Opposite this shop, turn right down Wijde Kerksteeg heading for the soaring tower of Oude Kerk.*

2 Oude Kerk

This lovely church (*see p47*) is encrusted with chapels and little houses tucked up against the walls. Ironically, too, it is hemmed in by sex cinemas and the windows of prostitutes who operate within metres of the city's oldest surviving monument. Oude Kerk (Old

Church) was founded in the 13th century; it contains 16th-century vault paintings and fine stained glass.
Return to Warmoesstraat, turn right and take the next street left.

3 Oudebrugsteeg

It is worth walking a short way down this alley to see the front of the Beurs van Berlage, and the Grasshopper Coffee Shop opposite.
Return to Warmoesstraat, turning left, and continue until the street ends. Look left for a good view of the station, then turn right in Zeedijk.

4 Zeedijk

The first house on the left, No 1, dates from 1550 and is one of only two medieval timber-framed houses left in Amsterdam. Opposite, the frieze above the doorway of St Olofskapel is carved with skeletons. At the first bridge, Oudezijds Kolk, the ancient lock still has its original gates and machinery.
Backtrack a short way from the bridge and turn left down Sint Olofssteeg, bearing left on to OZ Voorburgwal.

5 OZ Voorburgwal

Looking immediately to the left you will notice several 17th-century plaques, showing Noah's Ark and shipwrights' tools. Coming to the first bridge look right to No 14, De Leeuwenburgh, a fine example of a step-gabled house dating from 1605. A short way further down on the right is No 40, the Museum Amstelkring. The

attics of this and the two adjoining houses contain a *schuilkerk*, a clandestine Catholic church, dating from the 17th century. At the next bridge look back for a good view of St Nicolaaskerk with its neo-Baroque central dome. This harbourside church was built in 1885, shortly after the ban on Catholic worship in the city was lifted.
If you do not want to enter the red-light district, carry on up OZ Voorburgwal, past the Oude Kerk, to Damstraat, where you can turn right to return to Dam Square. Otherwise, continue over the bridge and on through Korte Niezel, then turn right on OZ Achterburgwal.

6 OZ Achterburgwal

This street is lined with sex shops, but looking upwards you will also see some of the city's most varied architecture. Many would like to see the area cleaned up and these charming buildings turned into apartments. As it is, property owners can make so much money by renting ground-floor rooms to prostitutes that they can afford to leave the rooms above unoccupied. For visitors who want to sample the area after dark, the Theatre Casa Rosso is one nightclub offering explicit erotic entertainment.
Turn right into Oude Doelenstraat and you will see the Koninklijk Paleis in Dam Square straight ahead. Alternatively, you can continue exploring the area by going on to the next walk (see p52).

The red-light district

Will I be safe? Will I be shocked? These two questions worry anyone entering Amsterdam's infamous red-light district. The answer to both is a qualified yes. Take precautions against theft and do not take photographs – there are plenty of gangland types about who want to remain anonymous, and your camera represents a threat. The shocks come more from the explicit contents of sex-shop windows than from the prostitutes themselves.

Despite the risks, the red-light district remains an essential part of the Amsterdam experience, as the large number of tour groups walking the area testify. As in every port city, commercialised sex has been available for centuries. Prostitutes operated here in the 17th century and paid rent to the city bailiff. He, therefore, had a vested interest in ensuring that they did not stray from the designated brothel area; if they did, he sent his drum and flute-playing guard to play outside the house in which they were ensconced until the combination of noise and exposure drove them back.

Not perhaps for every visitor, but Amsterdam's red-light district is undeniably a tourist attraction

Amsterdam prides itself on a tolerant attitude to sexual tastes

Today's red-light district is a pragmatic solution to a problem that will never go away. Under Dutch law, soliciting is illegal but what prostitutes and clients do in the privacy of their 'home' is regarded as their business – hence the *kamer te huur* signs (rooms to rent); officially the money that changes hands is room rent, not payment for services rendered.

The prostitutes have, in most cases, chosen this way of life for its easy money. If they change their minds, there are numerous church and government agencies willing to provide support. Drug dealing and the worst excesses of pornography are more recent phenomena which the police and city authorities are vigilantly trying to stamp out.

Since 2007, Amsterdam's red-light district has been more tightly regulated by the mayor and city council, and many operations have been closed down in an effort to improve the city's image. However, the curious visitor to this area will find there are still plenty of sights to be seen.

On the whole, the red-light district is colourful, it attracts tourists and contributes to the local economy, to the extent that brothel owners now sit on the Chamber of Commerce. There is a lighter side as well – the Condomerie Het Gulden Vlies (Golden Fleece) has benefited from the post-AIDS boom in condom demand; it sells every kind imaginable – edible, luminescent or explosive.

Bijbels Museum (Biblical Museum)

This specialised collection is devoted to the history of the Old and New Testaments and is an important research centre for Jewish and Christian scholars. The displays illustrate life in biblical times through archaeological material and reconstructions of key buildings, such as the Temple of Solomon. For many visitors the appeal is the house itself, with its stately period details, ceiling paintings by Jacob de Wit and two authentically furnished kitchens from the 17th century.

The house is part of a row (Nos 364 to 370) designed in 1662 by Philip Vingboons, one of the leading architects of the Golden Age. The builder was Jacob Cromhout who lived at No 366, hence its alternative name, the Cromhouthuisen. The lovely garden is an oasis in a busy city.

Herengracht 366–368. Tel: (020) 624 2436; www.bijbelsmuseum.nl.
Open: Mon–Sat 10am–5pm; Sun & public holidays 11am–5pm.
Closed: 1 Jan & 30 Apr. Admission charge. Tram: 1, 2 or 5. Nearby: Begijnhof.

De Burcht (Vakbondsmuseum) (National Trade Union Museum)

A museum devoted to the history of the Dutch trade union movement does not sound especially appealing but, like several other museums in Amsterdam, it is the building that makes a visit worthwhile. In this case the building is the work of the Amsterdam School pioneer, HP Berlage. Known as the

The Trade Union Museum is devoted to the working class

'Berlage Castle', it was commissioned in 1900 as the headquarters of the General Dutch Diamond Workers' Union.

Its exhibits, mainly photographs, and documents relating to the rise of the Dutch labour movement, are outshone by the magnificent stairwell, with its Art Deco stained glass, tiling, bas-reliefs and murals by Dutch Impressionist RN Roland Holst.

Henri Polaklaan 9. Tel: (020) 624 1166; www.deburcht-vakbondsmuseum.nl.
Open: Tue–Fri 11am–5pm, Sun 1–5pm.
Closed: Mon, Sat & public holidays.
Admission charge. Tram: 9 & 14. Nearby: Zoo (Artis), Hortus Botanicus Plantage (see pp130–31).

Churches

While fringe religions flourish in Amsterdam, from Hare Krishna to New Age anthroposophy, conventional church-going has declined, leaving many of the city's churches forlorn, locked and redundant. The three main churches can be visited, however, and all of them are monuments of significant historical and architectural importance worthy of the city's reverence.

Nieuwe Kerk (New Church)

Nieuwe Kerk, on Dam Square, is run by a foundation which has decided to utilise the church for art exhibitions, concerts, lectures and even antiques fairs. Even so, it remains the national church of the Netherlands, used for the investiture of monarchs.

The church was first built in 1408: it is 'new' only in the sense that it is 200 years younger than the Oude Kerk (Old Church). It was gutted by fire in 1645, hence its furnishings date from the Golden Age, including a fine Baroque pulpit of 1649 carved by Aelbert

The imposing Nieuwe Kerk on Dam Square

Vinckenbrink; a magnificent organ case designed by architect Jacob van Campen, an ornate bronze choir screen and elegant wooden pews. National heroes commemorated include Admiral Michiel de Ruyter (d. 1676) whose magnificent monument dominates the choir.
Dam Square. Tel: (020) 638 6909; www.nieuwekerk.nl. Open: 10am–5pm during exhibitions only (phone to check, or consult website). Tram: 1, 2, 4, 5, 9, 13, 14, 16, 17 & 24. Nearby: Koninklijk Paleis (see p55).

Oude Kerk (Old Church)

The city's oldest church was founded in the early 13th century. Pictures of ships feature everywhere, reminding us that the church is dedicated to St Nicolaas, the patron saint of sailors. The nave is ringed by numerous chapels sponsored by the city's powerful trade guilds. Richly coloured stained glass in the north choir, dating from 1555, depicts the Life of the Virgin. The door into the sacristy, where marriages were once certified, carries the motto: 'Wed in haste; repent at leisure'.

The tower has an especially tuneful carillon of bells, made in the 17th century, which is played every Saturday between 4pm and 5pm. You can climb the spire for views of the port and city.
Oudekerksplein 23. Tel: (020) 625 8284; www.oudekerk.nl. Open: Mon–Sat 11am–5pm, Sun 1–5pm. Closed: 25 Dec, 1 Jan and Queen's Day. Admission charge. Tram: 4, 9, 16, 24 & 25. Nearby: Amstelkring Museum (see pp26–7).

Westerkerk (West Church)

Westerkerk, built by Hendrik de Keyser in the early 17th century, is renowned for two things: Rembrandt's grave and the tower. Rembrandt was buried in an unmarked pauper's grave, rediscovered by archaeologists during recent restoration work.

The tower is the tallest in Amsterdam at 83m (276ft). It is topped by the gold, red and blue crown of the Habsburg Holy Roman Emperor, Maximilian I.

The city gained the right to display the imperial crown in its coat of arms in 1489. According to one story, the privilege was granted after Maximilian I was cured of an illness after visiting Amsterdam's shrine of the Sacred Host. Others, more cynically, say he gave away his crown as a measure of his indebtedness to Amsterdam's bankers.

Prinsengracht 281, corner of Westermarkt. Tel: (020) 624 7766; www.westerkerk.nl. Church open: Easter–Sept Mon–Fri 11am–3pm; Services: Sun 10.30am.
Tower open: Apr–Oct Mon–Sat 10am–5.30pm; Oct–Mar. Tours every half hour. Admission charge for tower.
Tram: 13, 14 & 17.
Nearby: Anne Frankhuis (see pp34–5).

Concertgebouw

Johannes Brahms, who conducted his Third Symphony in Amsterdam in 1879, is reputed to have told his hosts: 'You are good people but bad musicians'. The remark spurred the city to set about creating a permanent orchestra and concert hall, both of which have since achieved worldwide acclaim. The Concertgebouw building ranks as one of the top three concert halls in the world, alongside Vienna and Boston. The building was designed by AL van Gendt and opened in 1888, an elegant neoclassical structure with reliefs of the Muses and celestial musicians. After subsidence, the building was restored for its centenary in 1988, and given a new glass foyer.

The resident orchestra, the Koninklijk Concertgebouworkest, achieved international renown under Willem Mengelberg, Bernard Haitink and Riccardo Chailly and now under Mariss Jansons. Other top orchestras perform here, and the busy concert programme sometimes includes jazz as well as classics.

Concertgebouwplein 2–6. Tel: (020) 573 0460 (general enquiries); (020) 671 8345

Outside the Concertgebouw

(box office); www.concertgebouw.nl. The best way to see the interior is to attend a concert; free lunchtime recitals are given on Wed. Box office open: daily 10am–7pm. Tram: 3, 5, 12, 16 & 24. Bus: 170. Nearby: Rijksmuseum, Stedelijk Museum, Van Gogh Museum.

Electrische Museumtramlijn (Electric Tramline Museum)

The tram in the centre of Amsterdam seem to belong to another age, with their old-fashioned streetcar design and jangling bells. They are, however, youngsters compared to the 60 or so historic tram that have been gathered together from all over Europe to create this transport museum, which is understandably popular with children. Most of the trams are static but some are used (see times below) to provide a service from Haarlemmermeer station to Amsterdamse Bos (Amsterdam Woods, *see p130*). Here you can alight for a picnic, a walk or a visit to the playground, farm reserve or Bosmuseum (Woodland Museum, *see p130*). Alternatively you can continue on through the 800-hectare (1,977-acre) park to the tram terminus at Amstelveen, a total journey time of 30 minutes.

Haarlemmermeer station, Amstelveenseweg 264. Tel: (info) 0900 423 1100; www.museumtram.nl. Open: Easter–Oct, daily 11am–5pm. Tram: 16 (depart every 20–30 minutes from Haarlemmermeer station). Nearby: Amsterdamse Bos.

Heineken Browerij (Heineken Brewery)

A trip to the Heineken Brewery Museum (or Heineken Experience, as it is called nowadays) is more than just an indulgence for beer lovers; the former brewery has been turned into an excellent museum. The museum charts the invention of beer by the Sumerians, the origins of the first taverns and beer halls in Germany, the role of beer in festivities as depicted in the paintings of Brueghel and the vital importance of beer taxes to Amsterdam's medieval economy; vast quantities were consumed at the time simply because beer was a safer drink than water. Various parts of the brewing process are explained by audio-visual displays and the traditional white-tiled brewhouse is kept as spotless as it was when the brewery was operating.

Heineken finally closed the brewery in 1988 and relocated. It was a sad day for Amsterdam as beer had been brewed on the premises since 1592.

(continued on p54)

Heavy horses at the Heineken Museum

Jewish Amsterdam

The synagogue in the Gerard Doustraat

When Amsterdam was liberated from Nazi occupation on 5 May 1945, the city's Jewish population had fallen from 140,000 to fewer than 45,000. The

MR. VISSERPLEIN
CENTRUM
Mr. Dr. L E. VISSER (1871-1942)
RAADSHEER EN PRESIDENT HOGE RAAD DER NEDERLANDEN.
VERDEDIGDE DE BELANGEN VAN DE JOODSE BEVOLKING
TIJDENS DE DUITSE BEZETTING.

A plaque commemorates LE Visser, President of the Supreme Court of the Netherlands and key player in the Resistance movement

survivors had lost everything – family, friends and homes. These stark facts are brought home by a visit to Jodenbuurt, the former Jewish Quarter, where only a handful of pre-war buildings still remain standing.

Among the first refugees to arrive in Amsterdam at the beginning of the 17th century were Sephardic Jews, who had been expelled from Spain and Portugal for refusing to accept Christianity. They built the huge

Portuguese Synagogue (*see p53*) that dominates Mr Visserplein, between 1671 and 1675. Ashkenazic Jews from Germany and Poland soon followed; their synagogue complex on Jonas Daniël Meijerplein now houses the Jewish Historical Museum.

The statue of a burly dockworker stands between these two buildings. It was sculpted in 1952 by Marie Andriessen to commemorate a brave and singular act of defiance: in February 1941 the city's dockers and transport workers led a general strike in protest against Nazi treatment of the Jews. The strike, brutally suppressed, has gone down in Dutch history as the city's 'day beyond praise'.

Place names in the area perpetuate the memory of prominent Jews. Mr Visser was President of the Supreme Court of the Netherlands until he was dismissed by the Nazis; he played a prominent role in the Resistance until he died of natural causes. Jonas Daniël Meijer was a prominent 19th-century lawyer and a lifelong campaigner for Jewish civil rights.

Despite everything, Jews still play an important role in the city's life. The van Moppes family sought refuge in Brazil during the war. They later returned to found one of the city's best-known diamond companies, the firm of A van Moppes & Zoon.

Other important sights include: the Portuguese Synagogue, the Hollandsche Schouwburg, the Verzets (Resistance) Museum and the Auschwitz Memorial in Wertheim Park.

Inside the Jewish Historical Museum – a living exhibition of Jewish faith and history

Walk: Jodenbuurt

Amsterdam's Jewish Quarter has been redeveloped since World War II but it contains several notable monuments, including Rembrandt's house.

Allow 1 hour.

Take the Metro from Amsterdam Centraal Station and alight at the first stop, Nieuwmarkt.

1 Nieuwmarkt Metro

Protesters battled with police on 'Blue Monday', 24 March 1975, to prevent the demolition of Nieuwmarkt houses to make way for the Metro. Murals and a giant demolition ball in the station recall that event.

Take the exit marked Nieuwmarkt/Sint Antoniesbreestraat and turn left down the latter street.

2 De Pinto Huis

Number 69 Sint Antoniesbreestraat is an Italianate house dating from 1605; now a public library. Go in and look at the painted panels and ornate ceiling (*open: Mon & Wed 2–8pm, Fri 2–5pm, Sat 11am–4pm*). The house was built

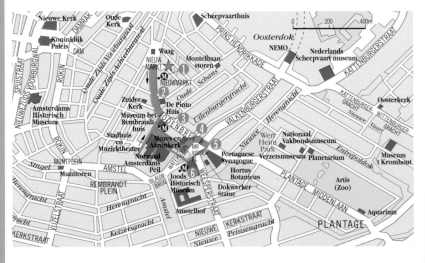

for Isaac de Pinto, a Jewish refugee who became a wealthy banker. Popular protest prevented this building from being demolished in the 1970s when the rest of the street was redeveloped. *Just beyond this house, on the left, is a lock called Sint Antoniessluis. Look left for a good view of the Montelbaanstoren, built in 1512 as part of the city's defences, and of the warehouses lining Oude Schans. Turn round and you will see Rembrandt's house.*

3 Museum het Rembrandthuis

This lovely house was built in 1606 (year of Rembrandt's birth) and cost the artist a huge 13,000 guilders when he bought it in 1639. Rembrandt was once hauled into court for cheating: he ordered wood to repair his house, and charged the cost to his neighbour, banker Isaac de Pinto. The banker sued, but the judge ruled that since de Pinto's name was on the bill, he must pay!
Turn right beside the Rembrandthuis, then left onto Waterlooplein where every day except Sunday you will find a flea market, a remnant of the old market of Jewish traders. Walk through the market to the church on the left.

4 Mozes en Aäronkerk

This vast neoclassical church dates from 1841 and many houses were demolished to make way for its construction.
Cross busy Mr Visserplein to the massive brick synagogue on the left.

5 Portuguese Synagogue

When completed in 1675, this Sephardic synagogue was the biggest in the world. The interior is untouched.
Cross Jonas Daniël Meijerplein (named after a remarkable lawyer who, at the age of 16 in 1796, became the first Jew to be admitted to the Dutch bar). Go to the synagogue complex opposite.

6 Joods Historisch Museum

The four buildings of the former Ashkenazic synagogue complex, now the Jewish Historical Museum, date from the mid-17th century.
Leave by the main entrance, walk down Turfsteeg and cross Waterlooplein to the Stadhuis, aiming for the glass-covered Normaal Amsterdams Peil arcade straight ahead.
Continue through the arcade. Turn left past the Muziektheater box office and Café Vienna. Leave the building by the doors straight ahead; look left at Blauwbrug, and right, down the Amstel, to Munttoren. Turn right for the black marble memorial slab for Jews who died in World War II. Follow Zwanenburgwal, alongside the Stadhuis, back to the Museum Het Rembrandthuis. The Metro entrance just ahead takes you back to Amsterdam Centraal Station.

NEARBY

Only a stone's throw from the Portuguese Synagogue, on Plantage Middenlaan, is the entrance to Hortus Botanicus Plantage, the Botanical Garden. Beyond, in the leafy suburb of Plantage, visitors will find Amsterdam's zoo, Natura Artis Magistra, known as Artis.

Walk: Jodenbuurt

Closure was inevitable as the Amsterdam plant could produce only 80,000 bottles an hour – less than Amsterdam alone consumes. The new plants have a staggering combined capacity of more than one million bottles an hour.

Stadhouderskade 78. Tel: (020) 523 9666; www.heinekenexperience.com. Open: Sept–May Tue–Sun 10am–6pm, June–Aug daily 11am–7pm. Admission charge. Tram: 7, 10, 16, 24 & 25. Nearby: Albert Cuypstraat (see p138).

ING Bank building

The head office of the former NMB-PostBank (now the ING Bank) is an intriguing and imaginative building, worth seeking out in its suburban location by those interested in new architectural trends. The building, the most expensive ever built in the Netherlands, was completed in 1987. It was designed by Ton Alberts and Max van Huut in accordance with anthroposophical principles, a New Age philosophy in vogue with Amsterdam intellectuals that has been described as combining western humanist values with elements from eastern religions.

The building is designed to be 'organic'; none of the walls meets at right angles, a rejection of the alienating box-like form of most office blocks. Critics describe the result as a giant sandcastle – admirers compare it to ancient Inca architecture. Running water is a feature – the sound intended to have a calming effect – and there are numerous courtyard gardens.

The ING Bank building stands in ironic counterpoint to the nearby tower blocks of Bijlmermeer *(see p11).*
Bijlmer 888. Tel: (020) 563 9111 (communication dept); www.ing.com. Open: sometimes possible to take a guided tour (for details, contact Archivisie). Tel: (020) 625 8908. Metro: Bijlmer.

Joods Historisch Museum (Jewish Historical Museum)

This museum is devoted to the history of the Jews in Amsterdam, a tragic story curtailed by the Nazi persecution of World War II. However, the museum is at pains to stress the continuity of Jewish life in the Netherlands.

The museum is housed in the former Ashkenazic synagogue complex, a series of 17th- and 18th-century buildings, and the displays cover three main themes. The first is concerned with the terror and persecution of the war, brought vividly to life by photographs and personal accounts. The second explains the Jewish religion, the major events in the calendar, its rituals and laws on diet and hygiene. Finally there is an account of the Jewish contribution to public life, politics and industry in Amsterdam, especially in developing the diamond industry.

The collection takes time to absorb, leaving visitors sober and reflective, but there is a lighter note – the excellent kosher café serves specialities such as almond *bolus* and *boterkoek* (buttercake). *Jonas Daniël Meijerplein 2–4. Tel: (020) 531 0310; www.jhm.nl. Open: Fri–Wed 11am–5pm, Thur 11am–9pm. Closed: Rosh Hashonah and Yom Kippur. Admission charge. Tram: 9 & 14.*

Koninklijk Paleis (Royal Palace)

The Royal Palace on Dam Square is Amsterdam's most prestigious architectural monument. It was built as an expression of civic pride between 1648 and 1655, when Amsterdam was at the peak of its power as a maritime trading city, capital of an empire stretching from the Americas to Australia.

Originally built as the Stadhuis or Town Hall, it was the one flamboyant structure in a city characterised by architectural restraint. There were practical reasons why Amsterdam had so few grandiose public buildings of any size: the soggy subsoil of mud and silt simply could not support any great weight of masonry.

The architect, Jacob van Campen, had to overcome this technical difficulty before he could fulfil his commission, to design the biggest town hall in all of Europe. He did so by creating a solid raft of timber piles, each 18m (59ft) deep. The precise number of the piles – 13,659 – is known to every Amsterdam schoolchild because of a simple formula: to the number of days in the year (365) add 1 in front, and 9 behind.

On top of this raft, van Campen built the huge neoclassical edifice whose main façades are 80m (262ft) long – just 2.13m (7ft) more than the town hall of Antwerp, up to then the biggest in Europe. Amsterdam further signalled its supremacy over Antwerp, the city that had once been its major rival in the competition for maritime trade, by placing the figure of Atlas holding up the globe on the west front pediment; below, all the nations of the world are depicted offering up their goods to an

(continued on p58)

Atlas shoulders the globe above the Royal Palace

Walk: The Golden Bend

The canal circle's Golden Bend was so named because of the size and splendour of the houses and the wealth of its former inhabitants.

Allow 1½ hours.

Begin on Dam Square. Walk to the left of the Koninklijk Paleis (Royal Palace) and cross the busy junction to walk down Raadhuisstraat.

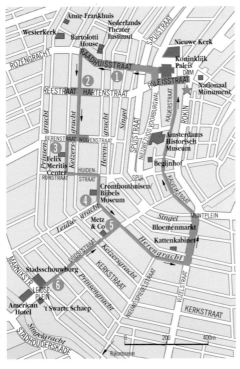

1 Raadhuisstraat

This street was laid out in 1894, cutting a broad swath through the canal circle. The magnificent 19th-century building on the right was the main Post Office until 1991 when it was converted to form the Magna Plaza shopping galleria. To the right, down Herengracht, is the ornate **Bartolotti House**, built in 1621 by Hendrik de Keyser. Next door is the Theatermuseum, dating from 1638. On the left-hand side of Raadhuisstraat is an attractive arcade designed by AL van Gendt, the same architect who built the Concertgebouw. *Turn left down Keizersgracht.*

2 The Nine Streets (Negen Straatjes)

As you walk, it is worthwhile exploring the nine short cross streets to right and left, linking the three main canals. Their names indicate that this part of

the city was once the haunt of furriers: *Reestraat* means Roe Street, *Harten* means deer, *Beren* bears.
After Berenstraat look for the building on the right inscribed 'Felix Meritis'.

3 Felix Meritis Center for Arts and Sciences

This neoclassical building was founded in 1788 as a lecture theatre and concert hall by the Felix Meritis Society, whose aim was to promote knowledge of the arts and sciences. Haydn, Brahms and Grieg all conducted here. From 1946 it was the headquarters of the Communist Party, which was well supported just after World War II for its role in the Resistance.
At the next bridge turn left down Huidenstraat, and right down Herengracht.

4 Cromhouthuisen/Bijbels Museum

Numbers 364 to 370 on the right derive their name from Jacob Cromhout, a builder whose trademark (shown on a plaque near the door to No 366) was a crooked stick, the literal meaning of his surname. Now the houses, dating from 1662, contain the Biblical Museum.
Continue down Herengracht. Stop to look at the succession of bridges marking the junction with Leidsegracht. Then take the first right, Leidsestraat.

5 Leidsestraat

A short way up on the right is Metz & Co, a department store founded in 1740. Despite its age, it sells ultra-chic modern fashion and furnishings.
Carry on up Leidsestraat to Leidseplein.

6 Leidseplein

This is the centre of Amsterdam nightlife, where its mixture of up-market establishments and cheap fast-food outlets has earned the square its nickname, 'La Place de la Mayonnaise'. On the right is the Stadsschouwburg (City Theatre). Alongside is the eccentric Art Nouveau **American Hotel**, built in 1904. Drop into the Café Americain to see its elegant stained glass, murals and chandeliers. On the left-hand side of the square is 't Swarte Schaep (The Black Sheep), a restaurant renowned for its Dutch-French cuisine. In the side streets to the right and left, respectively, are the city's two big rock music venues, Melkweg (at Lijnbaansgracht 234A) and Paradiso (at Weteringschans 6–8).
To return, backtrack down Leidsestraat and turn right down Herengracht. Turn left in Vijzelstraat to reach Muntplein, then follow Kalverstraat back to Dam Square.

NEARBY

From Leidseplein it is a short walk to the renowned Rijksmuseum where you can also join The Museum Quarter walk (*see pp68–9*). Simply turn left in Leidseplein, alongside 't Swarte Schaep restaurant, down Korte Leidsedwarsstraat, a street lined with cafés and restaurants. At the end you will see Museumbrug (Museum Bridge) to your right, leading to the Rijksmuseum.

Koninklijk Paleis, Amsterdam's most prestigious architectural monument

allegorical female figure representing the city of Amsterdam. By contrast, the weathervane on top of the central cupola depicts the humble Dutch Koggeschip – the Dutch Cog – one of thousands of sturdy merchant ships that roamed the world bringing back the spices and tropical produce that made the city so immensely rich.

A notable feature of the Stadhuis is the lack of a formal entrance; puzzled visitors often wander round the block several times before discovering the small concealed doorway (on the right-hand side of the portico facing on to Dam Square). There were good reasons for this: since the old city hall

was stormed in 1535 by rioting Anabaptists declaring the imminent end of the world, and strikes and demonstrations were a regular feature of city life, such concealment helped seal the building from rioters. Besides, the basement of the town hall contained the city's prison, arsenal and bank vaults – according to historian Mark Girouard, up to 16 million Dutch florins could be stored in the vault at any one time, 'a foundation every bit as impressive as the famous 13,659 timber piles'.

Thus, the town hall had to be impregnable and the entrance was deliberately built small.

On the other hand, the Stadhuis was a public building, open to anyone who cared to enter. The ground floor housed the courts and council chamber as well as the offices of various city charities responsible for managing orphanages and hospitals. The upstairs was largely empty. In their desire for the biggest and best, Amsterdammers got more space than they could actually use.

In 1808 Napoleon invaded the Netherlands and put his brother Louis on the throne. The Stadhuis was turned into the royal palace of today. As a result, the rooms contain an extensive collection of Empire furniture, but the most striking feature is the wealth of 17th-century marble sculpture, the work of Artus Quellin.

The sculpture is allegorical, indicating the use of each hall: Justice, Wisdom and Mercy decorate the tribunal or main courtroom; Venus is placed in the room where marriages were registered; and Icarus, falling from the sky, is in the office where merchants filed for bankruptcy. These playful and imaginative figures contrast with the more ponderous paintings that decorate the walls and ceilings, but even these provide an insight into key moments in the city's history and the moral values of the Golden Age.

Today the palace serves as a site to host royal events and is no longer a residence for Queen Beatrix, whose main home is in The Hague. It has been closed for renovation and is expected to open again in 2009.

Dam 1. Tel: (020) 620 4060; www.koninklijkhuis.nl. Telephone to check, or consult the website. Tram: 1, 2, 4, 5, 9, 13, 14, 16, 17, 24 & 25. Nearby: Nieuwe Kerk (see p47).

Madame Tussauds Amsterdam

If the Amsterdam Historical Museum is too dry for your tastes, try learning about the Golden Age of the Netherlands through the waxworks and tableaux of Madame Tussauds. In a romp through the 17th century, you will meet William of Orange and watch Rembrandt at work in his studio; enter a merchant's house, modelled on a painting by Vermeer, and watch children skating on the frozen canals of Amsterdam. Then the scene changes and you are back in the 20th century witnessing the first Moon walk and meeting famous politicians, pop stars and royalty. Interact with Captain Jack Sparrow, Robbie Williams or Ronaldinho – all good fun if it is a cold, wet day, or your children are bored with art and architecture.

Dam 20. Tel: (020) 522 1010;

Rembrandt at the Museum het Rembrandthuis

www.madame-tussauds.nl. Open: daily 10am–5.30pm (July–Aug 10am–8.30pm). Closed: 30 Apr. Admission charge. Tram: 1, 2, 4, 9, 13, 14, 16, 17, 24 & 25. Nearby: Koninklijk Paleis, Nieuwe Kerk, Amsterdams Historisch Museum (see pp32–3).

Museum het Rembrandthuis (Rembrandt House Museum)

The house in which Rembrandt spent the happiest and most successful years of his life is now a museum used to display an almost complete set of his etchings – 250 out of the 280 he is known to have made – along with drawings, personal memorabilia and period furniture. One room has an exhibition explaining the techniques of engraving, and the walls are hung with paintings by Rembrandt's pupils and by his teacher, Pieter Lastman.

The handsome Renaissance house was built in 1606. Rembrandt bought it in 1639, when he was 33 years old. He had previously lodged in the same street, having moved to Amsterdam from his native Leiden in 1631. He soon became an acclaimed artist, able to count on an income from major commissions. Even so, he borrowed heavily to buy, furnish and maintain the house. This, and his lack of business acumen, contributed to his bankruptcy in 1656. In 1658, his creditors forced him to sell the house, though he was allowed to continue living in it until 1660, when he moved to a cheaper home in the Jordaan district.

The house remains as it was in Rembrandt's day; the only subsequent change was the addition of a third storey with a classical pediment in place of the original step gable. Rembrandt and his household lived on the ground floor; the first floor served as his studio and the attic as the studio of his pupils. The house was then located on the edge of the city, in the fast-growing Jewish Quarter. Rembrandt chose the situation because the countryside was not far away. The museum was extended about ten years ago with the addition of a modern gift shop next to the Rembrandthuis.

The streets of the Jewish Quarter provided Rembrandt with a constant source of inspiration. His affection for low-life characters can be seen in the famous series of engravings, hung in this museum, of beggars, vagabonds, organ-grinders and rat-catchers – he even portrayed himself in the guise of a beggar.

Among the other pictures displayed are views of Amsterdam and the surrounding countryside, several revealing self-portraits and etchings of the artist's parents, his wife and their son, Titus. A visit to the toilets is a must just for Rembrandt's drawings of a woman squatting in the bushes and a man standing in a pose of evident relief! Jodenbreestraat 4. Tel: (020) 520 0400; www.rembrandthuis.nl. Open: daily 10am–5pm. Closed: 1 Jan. Admission charge. Tram: 9 & 14. Nearby: Joods Historisch Museum (see p54).

Rembrandt's life

Rembrandt Harmenszoon van Rijn was born in Leiden in 1606, the eighth child of a prosperous corn miller who owned a mill close to the River Rhine, hence the family name. Rembrandt studied for a career in the law until he gave up university to concentrate on art.

He moved to Amsterdam in 1631 and the following year received his first major commission, *The Anatomy Lesson of Dr Nicolaes Tulp* (now in the Mauritshuis Museum, The Hague),

One of the greatest artists of all time

portraying members of the city's guild of surgeons.

Fame and fortune followed, but so did personal tragedy. His wife, Saskia, died in 1642; three of their four children died in early childhood, leaving only Titus, whom Rembrandt adored. In that same year, despite Saskia's death, Rembrandt painted his best-known picture, *The Night Watch*.

This occupies the position of honour in the Rijksmuseum, but it was criticised in its time because some faces in the picture are partially hidden – the realism we value was condemned at the time and his critics further accused Rembrandt of not following the 'rules of art', instead pursuing his own private insights.

He began to receive fewer commissions and, in 1656, was declared bankrupt. In 1660, he moved to a modest dwelling in Jordaan. Here he painted some of his greatest works, including the glowing and mysterious *The Jewish Bride* (Rijksmuseum). The sickly Titus died, aged 27, in 1668 and Rembrandt followed him less than a year later. In October 1669, he was buried in an unmarked pauper's grave (recently rediscovered) in Westerkerk, an ignominious end for one of Amsterdam's dearest sons.

A sea-dog's paradise at the Kromhout Museum

Museumwerf 't Kromhout (Museum Shipyard)

The Kromhout Works is the only remaining shipyard of the many that once filled Amsterdam's eastern harbour. Today it concentrates on restoring historic vessels.

The 'working museum' was founded in the 18th century by Diede Jansen Kromhout. It specialised in building iron vessels in the 19th century. The ornate glass and iron canopy that stands over the original slipway now shelters the working part of the museum where visitors can watch boats and engines being repaired.

The adjoining display area features models of steamers, shipwrights' tools and engravings of the docks in their heyday.

Hoogte Kadijk 147. Tel: (020) 627 6777; www.machinekamer.nl. Open: Tue

10am–3pm. Admission charge. Bus: 22 & 32. Nearby: Nederlands Scheepvaartmuseum (Dutch Maritime Museum); Docklands.

Nederlands Scheepvaartmuseum

The Netherlands Maritime Museum is housed in a massive building on the waterfront which was built in 1656 as the warehouse and arsenal of the Amsterdam Admiralty. Here the provisions of the Dutch navy were stored. The Admiralty employed a huge task force of cats whose job was to patrol the stores looking for rats and mice. The museum closed in 2007 for an extensive renovation and will reopen in 2009. Please consult *www.scheepvaartmuseum.nl* for more information.

The sheer size and scale of the building can be judged by the fact that it now accommodates several very large historic vessels, as well as evocative paintings, maps and globes, all of which help tell the story of the Dutch maritime achievement; the story is covered exhaustively, from ancient Roman ships to luxurious modern passenger liners and leisure craft.

Perhaps the most interesting part of the museum covers the Golden Age. The first Dutch expeditions to the Spice Islands – modern Indonesia – set sail in the 1590s. Their aim was to chart navigable routes to the East Indies, via the Cape of Good Hope and the Indian Ocean. Reliable sea maps underpinned the rapid rise of the Netherlands as a trading nation. Among collectors of early maps, the names of Dutch cartographers such as Blau and Jansson are held in reverence for the accuracy and beauty of their work. The maps and globes displayed in the Maritime Museum are equally fascinating because they show, step by step, the charting of hitherto unexplored islands and continents such as Australia (then called New Holland), Tasmania, China, Japan and the coast of South America.

Amsterdam's shipbuilders also led the world, which is why Sir Walter Raleigh, Samuel Pepys and Tsar Peter the Great all visited, looking for ideas that would benefit the English and Russian navies. The museum explains the development of the sturdy three-masted merchant vessels of the 16th century which sailed in search of spices and luxury goods and

The East Indiaman *Amsterdam*, which will be available to view in a temporary location throughout the Maritime Museum's renovation

of the powerful warships of the Dutch fleet used to defend the nation's commercial interests.

The first merchant voyages were financed by private entrepreneurs who, in the main, reaped a rich reward. In 1602 it was decided that Far East trade should be co-ordinated, and numerous small companies joined forces to create the Dutch East India Company. This was funded by an innovative public share flotation and the company's charter gave it almost unlimited powers.

By 1669 it was synonymous with Dutch colonial power; it employed a private army and owned a huge fleet of warships and merchant vessels, having established trading outposts stretching from South Africa to the Japanese island of Deshima.

The Dutch West India Company was founded in 1621 with similar powers, to co-ordinate trade with West Africa and the Americas. It was less successful, suffering intense competition from the English, Spanish and Portuguese.

One of its colonies, established on the island of Manhattan, was captured by the English in 1664, and its name changed from New Amsterdam to New York.

The museum's account of the rise and fall of these two powerful trading companies is fascinating, but there are plenty of other diversions. Children especially will admire the gilded royal barge (made in 1818 for King William I), and the reconstructed East Indiaman *Amsterdam*, moored in the dock outside the museum, is alone worth the price of the entrance ticket. Climbing aboard this ship, whose crew consists of actors, you gain a very real sense of the bravery of sailors who plied the oceans in such a vulnerable construction of wood and sailcloth. During the renovation, the East Indiaman *Amsterdam* will be moored by the science centre NEMO and remain open to the public. Purchase tickets at NEMO.

Kattenburgerplein 1.
www.scheepvaartmuseum.nl.
Open: Tue–Sun & public holidays
10am–5pm, mid-June–mid-Sept daily
10am–5pm. Closed: 1 Jan, 30 Apr & 25
Dec. Admission charge. Bus: 22 & 32.
Nearby: Docklands, Museumwerf 't
Kromhout.

NEMO

NEMO, the national science centre, is located in a striking building designed by Italian architect Renzo Piano. Young and old visitors alike can learn hands-on about the fascinating world of science and technology. There are five floors of permanent and changing exhibitions about how the world works… where you can smell, hear, see and feel.

Oosterdok 2, near the IJ Tunnel entrance.
Tel: (020) 531 3233; www.e-nemo.nl.
Open: Tue–Sun 10am–5pm (and Mon
during school holidays June–Aug).
Admission charge. Bus: 22. Nearby:
Nederlands Scheepvaartmuseum.

Rijksmuseum

The Rijksmuseum is one of Amsterdam's major highlights. The museum building is a vast neo-Gothic palace with Burgundian towers and sculptural reliefs, designed by PJH Cuypers and completed in 1885. The national art collection of the Netherlands is in this museum, which contains a treasure-house of paintings, applied art, porcelain, silver and Asiatic sculpture. The museum is far too big to absorb in one visit: it pays to be selective.

The Rijksmuseum is currently being renovated and much of it will be closed until 2010. However, about 400 of the highlights are still being shown in a special 'masterpieces' display in the Philips Wing, including many of the works covered in the following pages. The description here is based on the museum as it was when it was closed. When it reopens in 2010, the layout will be different, but it is not yet possible to say what it will be like.

Rembrandt

For many visitors the Rijksmuseum means one painting, Rembrandt's celebrated *The Night Watch. The Night Watch* was named in the 19th century when experts believed the painting depicted a night scene. The layers of soot-blackened varnish have since been removed to reveal a quite different picture in which Rembrandt's dramatic use of sunlight and shade can be fully appreciated. Despite restoration, the old name has stuck, partly because the now-accepted title, *The Militia Company of Captain Frans Banning Cocq,* is such a mouthful.

The painting is an official portrait of one of the militia companies which acted as a combined police force-cum-army, ensuring law and order in the city and taking it in turns to mount a guard at the city gates. Each company had its own clubhouse and wealthier members paid for group portraits to adorn the walls. Hundreds of such portraits – the equivalent of today's group photographs – have survived, including those that hang in the Civic Guard Gallery of the Amsterdam Historical Museum.

Rembrandt's innovation was to break away from the static banquet scene or formal pose to show the militia company in action. Captain Cocq is giving his men the order to set off on a patrol of duty. He and his lieutenant are lit by a pool of sunlight while the militiamen behind are shown emerging from the shadowy gate of their clubhouse. The painting is full of movement as the men shoulder their weapons and form up into marching line, the dynamism enhanced by the play of light and the little girl caught up in the disorder. Her presence in the picture is a mystery; it is suggested that she may have been the daughter of the landlord of the militia clubhouse. The dead rooster hanging from her belt is an enigmatic pun (perhaps with bawdy connotations) on the name of Captain Cocq.

Rembrandt's contemporaries were not universally impressed by this work; some hailed it as a masterpiece of realism but far more censured him for failing in his fundamental duty as a portraitist to show the faces of each militiaman clearly. Instead, several faces are obscured by gesturing arms or shadow.

Further Rembrandt works include two self-portraits – one painted at the age of 22, the other (*Self-Portrait as the Apostle Paul*) in 1661 after bankruptcy had forced a major change in his lifestyle. In the same year, he painted the arresting *Bridal Pair*, also known as *The Jewish Bride*, a tender portrait of an unknown couple in glowing and heavily impasted reds and golds. Another masterpiece, *De Staalmeesters*, depicts five inspectors of the Drapers' Guild and a hatless servant. From the way they look out of the picture it has been suggested that they are portrayed at a public meeting – someone in the invisible audience has addressed an unexpected question to them and their expressions, brilliantly highlighted by the muted black of their clothes, range from bemused tolerance to a rather lofty contempt.

Tower Mill at Wijk bis Duursteede by the artist Jacob van Ruysdael is just one of the masterpieces in the Rijksmuseum's collection

During renovation the visitor's entrance is around the corner from the museum, to the right. (*Jan Luijkenstraat 1*). Note: in recent years, a small gallery of the Rijksmuseum can be visited at Schiphol Airport, just near passport control, for departing passengers. No charge.
Stadhouderskade 42. Tel: (020) 674 7047; www.rijksmuseum.nl. Open: daily 9am–6pm. Closed: 1 Jan. Admission charge. Tram: 2, 5, 7, 10, 16, 24 & 25. Nearby: Stedelijk Museum, Van Gogh Museum (see p84). For information updates on the opening in 2010, please see website: www.rijksmuseum.nl

The Golden Age

Apart from the works of Rembrandt, the Rijksmuseum is noted for its collection of 17th-century works painted during the period of peace and prosperity known as the Golden Age of the Netherlands. For instance in the lively portrait of *Isaac Massa and his Wife* by Frans Hals the tubby and prosperous Isaac Massa leans back as if to show off his neat smiling wife, a paragon of fidelity as symbolised by the ivy clinging to the tree behind.

Hendrick Avercamp's *Winter Landscape* and Jacob van Ruysdael's *Tower Mill at Wijk bis Duursteede* are superb examples of the landscape painting for which Dutch artists are renowned.

Many of Jan Steen's witty genre paintings depict the artist himself and his family in scenes of wild abandon, illustrating popular moralistic proverbs of the age – for example, *homo bulla*, or 'man is a bubble'. At first sight, *The Merry Family* looks like a happy domestic scene until you notice that the children are smoking, drinking and being as licentious as their parents. The motto above the fireplace provides an ironic commentary; it says the young will sing the same old song, meaning that parents should beware of setting a bad example.

Quite different in tone altogether are the exquisite works of the Delft School, including four paintings by Vermeer and several by Pieter de Hooch. These simple paintings radiate peace and tranquillity, lending spiritual significance to the dutiful performance of the most ordinary domestic activities.

Dutch history and Asiatic art

Works that illustrate important aspects of Dutch history, even though they have no special artistic merit, include portraits of key figures, such as William of Orange, historic battles at sea and on land, scenes of everyday life in the 17th century and, most fascinating of all, relics of colonial life in the East Indies, Ceylon, China and Japan.

Visit the Asiatic art collection in the basement of the Philips Wing. Here, among Indonesian sculptures and Hindu-Javanese architectural fragments, is the arresting figure of *Shiva, Lord of the Dance*, surrounded by a ring of fire. This 12th-century bronze from southern India is as stunning a work in its own way as the paintings upstairs, yet it receives far fewer visitors. The section ends with a comprehensive display of Chinese ceramics and some beautifully embroidered Japanese textiles.

Sculpture and applied art

This collection is organised chronologically, beginning with medieval and Renaissance art. Some of the best exhibits consist of Romanesque and Gothic sculpture rescued from various abbeys and churches in the Netherlands. For fans of Delftware, there is a wealth of examples, including novelty items such as a birdcage, a violin and a pair of high-heeled shoes.

A staircase leads to the ground floor where you may have to queue to get close to the popular doll's houses made in the 18th century with exquisite attention to detail. The remaining rooms illustrate Dutch interior design in the 18th and 19th centuries. This theme continues in the little-visited basement which is worth seeking out for its outstanding collection of Empire and Art Nouveau furniture.

Later Dutch art

Paintings of the 18th to the early 20th century are displayed in the ground-floor Drucker Extension. Most rewarding are the Impressionistic works of The Hague and Amsterdam Schools hung in the last three rooms – notably the atmospheric pictures of Amsterdam street life at the beginning of the 20th century painted by George Hendrick Breitner.

The Doll's House of Petronella Oortman, which the Rijksmuseum estimates cost its owner as much as a real house along one of Amsterdam's canals at the time

Art in the Golden Age

John Evelyn, Samuel Pepys and other visitors to 17th-century Amsterdam were amazed by the quantity of fine art on sale. The first truly open market for art developed here, sold through dealers, bookshops and auctioneers. Instead of art being the preserve of rich patrons and institutions, ordinary citizens could commission portraits of their houses, possessions, friends or even of their prize animals (see Paulus Potter's *The Young Bull* in the Mauritshuis Museum, The Hague). Amsterdammers were particularly fond of paintings with a coded message. Understanding the symbolism reveals that many of the Rijksmuseum's pictures are far more complex than they seem on the surface. Dogs, for example, represent gluttony and licentiousness, reflecting

De Melkmeid (*The Milkmaid*) by Johannes Vermeer, 1658

Rembrandt's *The Night Watch* at the Rijksmuseum

on the behaviour of the people in the picture. Golden vases, cut-glass decanters, musical instruments and peacock feathers represent vanity. The frailty of human fortune is symbolised by eggshells or a fallen glass. Sometimes the paintings contain verbal puns: *vogelen*, the verb made of the noun '*vogel*' (bird), is similar to the slang term for copulation, hence a man holding up a dead pheasant is saying more than you might at first suspect.

The paintings of the age therefore work in two ways; as representations of everyday life and as serious moral works. Jan Steen's bawdy tavern scenes in the Rijksmuseum are a warning against loose morals. Another of his works in the same museum has a seemingly innocuous title – *The Toilet* – yet it is full of erotic allusions: the phallic candlestick, the sleeping dog, the red stockings (traditionally the symbol of a prostitute) and the open jewellery box. Amsterdammers would know well how to read this as a warning against the prostitution of moral principles for mercenary ends.

Walk: The Museum Quarter

This walk combines Amsterdam's three major museums with the best of the city's up-market shopping.

Allow 1½ hours.

Start at the Rijksmuseum. This is served by tram 2, 5, 7 and 10, but a more enjoyable way to reach it is by Museumboat (departures every 30 or 45 minutes from 10am to 5pm daily from in front of Amsterdam Centraal Station; see also pp181–2).

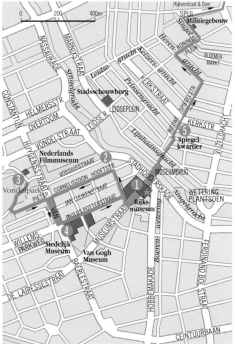

1 Rijksmuseum

Intended as a 'cathedral of the arts', the museum was built in neo-Gothic style in 1885 and embellished with sculptures and murals.

The vast collection inside was begun in the 18th century and later given impetus by Louis Napoleon, who set up the Grand Musée Royal in the Koninklijk Paleis in a bid to make Amsterdam a major centre for the arts.

Today the collection consists of 17 million works of art, although only 400 are currently on display during renovation. *Walk under the echoing tunnel beneath the Rijksmuseum and turn right. Cross Jan Luijkenstraat and turn left on to Pieter Corneliszoon Hooftstraat.*

2 PC Hooftstraat

At Amsterdam's most elegant shopping street, Dutch celebrities and the wealthy elite come to buy designer labels. This street has snob appeal and little soul, but can be amusing for its annual 'stiletto race', where brave women sprint in shoes over 10cm (4in) high.
After crossing Van Baerlestraat, continue up PC Hooftstraat to enter Vondelpark.

3 Vondelpark

This green oasis in the centre of the city was laid out in 1865 and named after the 17th-century Dutch poet, Joost van den Vondel, known as the 'Shakespeare of the Netherlands'.

There are plenty of outdoor concerts throughout the summer. The Nederlands Filmmuseum, a popular venue showing a wide selection of 'art' and historic films, has just announced plans to relocate at the end of 2009 to a modern new building across the water behind Centraal Station. The building in the Vondelpark will remain open until 2009. Call for programmes and opening hours.
Tel: (020) 589 1400; www.filmmuseum.nl. Retrace your steps down Van Baerlestraat. Take the second left, Paulus Potterstraat, for the other two big museums.

4 Stedelijk Museum and Van Gogh Musuem

The Stedelijk Museum normally houses the city's collection of modern art, and plans to reopen in a modern structure on this site at the end of 2009. A temporary site by Centraal Station is in operation at the time of going to press. Visit *www.stedelijk.nl* for details.

Unlike the Stedelijk, the Van Gogh Museum is stark and ultra-modern. It was designed by Gerrit Rietveld and completed in 1973. Van Gogh's vibrant paintings inside are far more colourful.
Continue down Paulus Potterstraat past Coster Diamonds (whose workshops can be visited daily 9am–5pm). Turn right, then left, passing through the Rijksmuseum tunnel. Cross the busy Stadhouderskade to reach Museumbrug (Museum Bridge) and head straight on for the Spiegelkwartier.

5 The Spiegelkwartier

This area can be considered an extension of the Museum Quarter but with a difference: the works of art are all for sale. Every shop along Spiegelgracht, Nieuwe Spiegelstraat and Kerkstraat is full of treasures and you can browse for hours.
Continue to the end of Nieuwe Spiegelstraat, past the Stichting de Appel, centre for modern art (temporary exhibitions open: Tue–Sun 11am–6pm; admission charge), then turn left on Herengracht. Take the first right, Koningsplein, which passes the floating flower market on the right. Bear left along Singel to see No 425, the Militiegebouw (Militia Building), built in 1660 as the city arsenal and now the University Library. Take the next right, Spui, and the next left, Kalverstraat, to return to Dam Square.

Walk: Jordaan

*Jordaan is the sock-shaped district wrapped round the western half of the canal circle. Despite its name (*jordaan *is a 'bastardised' version of the French* jardin, *meaning garden, and many streets are named for plants and flowers), this was the industrial quarter of 17th-century Amsterdam where noxious trades were carried on. Once working class, it is now a more upmarket neighbourhood of shops and cafés, and numerous hidden almshouses (*hofjes).

Allow 1½ hours.

From Dam Square walk down Raadhuisstraat past Westerkerk and over the bridge to the left bank of Prinsengracht. Walk down this canal and take the second left, Bloemgracht.

1 Bloemgracht

The Flower Canal is also known as the Herengracht (Gentlemen's Canal) of the Jordaan because it has the most splendid houses. The step-gabled buildings, Nos 87–91, date from 1642.
At the second bridge turn right into Tweede Leliedwarsstraat.

2 Tweede Leliedwarsstraat

Craft shops and art galleries line this short street.
Cross Nieuwe Leliestraat and take the next left.

3 Egelantiersgracht

The beautifully named Eglantine (Honeysuckle) Street has a well-restored almshouse, Sint Andrieshofje, at Nos 107–114, dated 1617, one of the oldest in the city. Enter to see a remarkable Delft-tiled passageway with a hidden garden. From outside the building turn round and walk up the canal, noting the plaques of No 89, two tailors at work, and Nos 61–3, a hooded hawk. Plaques like these, often relating to the householder's profession, were once used to identify houses.

At the next bridge look right for a good view of Westerkerk, then turn left down Tweede Egelantiersdwarsstraat. There are scores of excellent shops along this street. Turn right in Egelantiersstraat and look for the almshouse entrance at No 52.

4 Claes Claeszoon Hofje

This almshouse consists of 23 smaller houses dating from 1620 which display a fine sequence of gable styles.

Turn left in Eerste Egelantiersdwarsstraat and left again in Tuinstraat. Halfway up on the left is Regensboog-Liefdehofje, with 17th-century step gables. Take the next right, Tweede Tuindwarsstraat, cross Anjelierstraat (Carnation Street) then continue down ze Anjelierdwarstraat and

Old houses border the quiet Egelantiersgracht

Tichelstraat, and turn right in Karthuizerstraat.

5 Huys Zillen Weduwen Hofje

This street is dominated by the long façade of the 1650 almshouse – the 'House of the Elderly Widows'.

Return to Tichelstraat, looking left for a last view of Westerkerk. Turn right onto Lijnbaansgracht and walk down this canal, past the iron lifting bridge on Willemsstraat. Turn right in Palmgracht.

6 Palmgracht

Here are several more fine houses. Nos 73–79, on the right, date from 1673, and their plaque depicts a bunch of radishes. On the left, at Nos 28–38, is the Boffschehofje, founded in 1648 by Pieter Adriaenszoon Raep, whose surname means turnip, hence the vegetable depicted on the plaque.

At the end of Palmgracht turn right on to Brouwersgracht. Follow this canal, with its numerous bridges, boats and waterfowl, all the way back to the centre of Amsterdam, heading for the copper-green dome of the Lutheran Round Church (see p36) visible in the distance.

HOFJES

Many of the *hofjes* in the Jordaan district were built by wealthy merchants for housing sick or retired employees and their families. The pensioners were expected to work in return for this charity and the characteristic inner courtyard was originally used as a *bleekveld*, a bleaching field, for laying out cloth to bleach in the sun. Many are now beautifully planted communal gardens.

Marketplace of the world

Dutch maritime expansion in the 17th century turned Amsterdam into the world's biggest market for tropical goods. Contemporary visitors wrote of the harbour bustling with hundreds of ships so that they first glimpsed the city through a forest of masts and rigging. Timber causeways and floating wooden cranes stretched far out into the harbour. Strangers arriving after dark, when they were not allowed into the city, were lodged in one of two purpose-built floating inns. Visitors were impressed by the sheer noise of the Beurs, the commodities exchange, where Muscovites, Persians, Turks,

The Schreierstoren (Tower of Tears)

Most of the city's elegant canalside houses and warehouses were built in the 17th century; the hoists are still necessary for moving furniture, since the buildings only have narrow staircases

West Indians and traders from scores of other nations haggled over the price of sugar and spices, silks and Chinese porcelain. The city's own merchants were helped by the Bank of Amsterdam, founded in 1609, which offered loans at rates of only three or four per cent interest. With this ready source of cheap money, merchants could speculate, buying goods cheap and warehousing them until prices rose.

Warehouses remain the most visible legacy of the era. Though since turned into apartments, many retain their huge shuttered doors and pulley wheel in the gable. A maze of pipes inside carried water from rooftop cisterns for use in the event of fire – the origin of modern sprinkler systems. There are other reminders of the era in the palatial headquarters of the Dutch East India Company and the Schreierstoren (Tower of Tears), where sailors took leave of their wives and girlfriends before departing overseas. Sadly, though, Amsterdam lost its maritime atmosphere in the 1880s when the old harbour was filled in to build Centraal Station, thus signalling the end of the city's long and profitable relationship with the sea. The lower level of the Schreierstoren operates as a café and is a splendid historical structure.

Spaarndammerburt

The Spaarndammerburt housing estate is one of the most characteristic examples of the work of the famous Amsterdam School, a group of idealistic architects who worked in the city from 1911 to 1923. Their work was stimulated by the 1901 Housing Act under which the municipality was empowered to build subsidised 'council housing'.

This group of architects responded with distinctive and ornamental buildings, a far cry from the box-like housing units of a later age. One of their fundamental beliefs was that the

AMSTERDAM'S NEW SOUTH

Many of the buildings in the Nieuw Zuid (New South) were designed in the distinctive Amsterdam School style by Michel de Klerk and Pieter Kramer. If you like this style of architecture, take tram 4 from Centraal Station, alight at Rooseveltlaan and explore the triangular area bounded by Churchillaan to the north (the rather ugly 12-storey block in the apex of the triangle has the dubious honour of being Amsterdam's first skyscraper, built in 1935).

Another oasis of playful Amsterdam School work is the estate called De Dageraad (The Dawn), completed in 1923. To find it, continue north from Churchillaan, up Waalstraat, to PL Taakstraat.

A building in Amsterdam's New South

Sculpture at the Muziektheater

souls of the working-class occupants should be stimulated by presenting them with architecture of great aesthetic beauty.

The buildings of Spaarndammerburt make great use of deep sweeping roofs of terracotta tile, of patterned brickwork, sculpture and whimsical detail. The needle-like spire rising from the buildings on Hembrugstraat serves no purpose other than to enliven the roofscape. Straight lines are avoided in favour of gracious curving façades and window frames, giving the buildings a ship-like appearance. The architects planned every detail, down to the letter boxes and the type-style used for house numbering. These photogenic buildings are a joy to visit – modern, yet reminiscent of the intimate *hofjes*, or enclosed courtyards, of medieval Amsterdam.

Spaarndammerburt lies to the northwest of the Jordaan district. The best buildings are bounded by Zaanstraat, Hembrugstraat and Oostzaanstraat. Bus: 22. Nearby: the Western Islands (see Unknown Amsterdam, *pp92–3).*

Stadhuis/Muziektheater Complex

These public buildings, on the edge of the abruptly redeveloped Jewish Quarter, are known to Amsterdammers as the Stopera complex – a contraction of Stadhuis (City Hall) and Opera, but also an ironic reference to the 'Stop the Opera' campaign of the 1970s and early 1980s. Controversy surrounded these buildings from the start because of the cost (300 million guilders, which activists would have preferred to see spent on housing and other social needs), the inclusion of an opera, and ballet theatre (regarded as elitist) and the fact that numerous houses which had been taken over by squatters were demolished to clear the site.

Despite violent protests, the buildings went ahead and were completed in 1988. The controversy lingers, but in more muted form; critics regard the complex as an ugly eyesore that is out of scale with the surrounding canalside houses. The **Muziektheater**, with its white marble cladding, is dismissively nicknamed 'the set of dentures'. It is home to the Netherlands Opera and National Ballet companies, but continues to be dogged by poor acoustics, despite expensive attempts to remedy the problem.

Visitors to Amsterdam should see the complex – indeed, it is hard to miss – and make up their own mind. You can take advantage of free lunchtime concerts given between September and June. From the inside the huge plate-glass windows frame superb views.

The arcade linking the two parts of the complex has a mural showing a cross-section through the Netherlands to illustrate Normaal Amsterdams Peil (Normal Amsterdam Level), the standard ordnance datum by which heights are measured in this country where half the land lies below sea level.

Muziektheater: Amstel 3. Tel: (020) 625 5455 (box office); www.muziektheater.nl. Open: daily 10am till performance starts, Sun & public holidays from 11.30am. Guided tours: Sat 3pm. Free admission but there is a charge for guided tours (book in advance for English-language version). Stadhuis: Amstel 1. Tel: (020) 552 9111. Guided tours first Mon of the month at 11am. Admission charge. Tram: 9 & 14. Nearby: Waterlooplein Flea Market (see p138), Museum Het Rembrandthuis.

Displays at the Stedelijk Museum are currently in storage

Stedelijk Museum

Amsterdam's modern art museum has always been a great complement to the other two main museums in the Museum Quarter, the Rijksmuseum and the Van Gogh Museum. However, the building, which dates back to 1895, is at present being renovated, and with the Rijksmuseum partially closed, the Museum Quarter has been effectively halved.

As we went to press, the best of the Stedelijk's collection was still on display at its temporary home in the old post office building near Centraal Station, the Post CS, which is itself in the process of being redeveloped.

The Stedelijk's new home won't be ready for occupation until 2009, and it may well move to another temporary home at some point, so visitors will need to see the website for the latest information: *www.stedelijk.nl*

One reason for the renovation is to make better use of the space, as there has never been room to show more than a part of the collection, which covers the period from 1850 to the present day. Many of the big names in modern art are represented, though not always with well-known works. These in themselves often shed new light on a particular artist to the average visitor not thoroughly familiar with their life's work.

Names such as Cézanne, Chagall, de Kooning, Lichtenstein, Matisse, Mondrian, Picasso and Warhol all draw the crowds, but often it is the more striking examples of contemporary works which catch the eye. One of the permanent exhibits has always been a room devoted to the work of the Russian artist, Kasimir Malevich. The works were chosen by the artist himself and the accompanying text explains his personal evolution from realism, through cubism to Suprematism, a form of art that is concerned with the essence of colour, form and technique rather than representation. It will be interesting to see how these, and the other great works from the collection, are displayed in the new building.
Temporary home: Post CS (2nd & 3rd floors), Oosterdokskade 5.
There is a café on the 11th floor.
Tel: (020) 573 2911.
Tram: 1, 2, 4, 5, 9, 13, 16, 17, 24 & 25.
Permanent home: Paulus Potterstraat 13.
For information about opening, consult the website: www.stedelijk.nl.
Tram: 2, 3, 5 & 12.

Theatermuseum

The Theatre Museum is housed in a splendid 17th-century building, which is worth seeing in its own right. The house was purchased in 1638 by Michael Pauw, founder of the Dutch West India Company, and transformed by the leading Golden Age architect, Philip Vingboons. For the façade of the building, Vingboons designed the first ever 'neck gable', so-called because of its resemblance to the neck and shoulders of a wine bottle. The device was to prove popular and was widely copied by other Amsterdam architects.

The Theatre Museum

The murals and ceiling paintings of the interior, depicting landscapes and biblical subjects, date from a refurbishment in 1728, and are the work of the leading artists of their day, Jacob de Wit and Isaac de Moucheron. These are complemented by lavish stucco work and a magnificent spiral staircase.

The museum itself tells the history of Dutch theatre from the 17th century up to the modern age of TV, film and video, through a range of fascinating changing exhibits. These include a miniature theatre dating from 1781, a fine costume collection, props, books, drawings, prints, models illustrating the backstage work of scenery, lighting and stage effects, including wind, rain and thunder machines. There is also a garden where tea is served, a popular meeting place for actors, writers and directors.

Herengracht 168. Tel: (020) 551 3300; www.tin.nl. Open: Mon–Fri 11am–5pm, Sat–Sun & public holidays 1–5pm. Closed: 1 Jan, 30 Apr & 25 Dec. Admission charge. Tram: 13 & 17. Bus: 21.

Tropenmuseum (Tropical Museum)

The Tropical Museum is housed in one of the city's most charming buildings, the former Dutch Colonial Institute, a whimsical structure of minaret-like towers designed in the 'eclectic' style and completed in 1923. The façades are decorated with reliefs depicting the peoples of the East, the cultivation of the most important crops of the former colonies – rubber, tobacco, sugar and rice – and four of the major world religions, Hinduism, Islam, Christianity and animism, the belief that inanimate and natural phenomena have souls.

The museum was transformed in the 1970s from a celebration of Dutch imperialism to something altogether more exciting. The museum now illustrates life in the tropics and subtropics: India, Southeast Asia and South America are brought to life through colourful and authentic reconstructions of huts, houses, bazaars

A colourful display at the Tropical Museum

and shops, complete with characteristic smells; only the heat and flies are missing, and background tapes play continuously to evoke the noise and bustle of the streets.

Visitors wander in and out of the displays making their own discoveries. One minute you are wending your way through crowded Arab alleyways, the next you are out on the African savannah, caught in a thunderstorm. It is easy to lose yourself for hours, especially if you settle down to watch some of the documentary video tapes dealing with problems in the developing world, such as rainforest depletion and population growth.

The museum hosts numerous cultural events and also has a theatre, the Soeterijn, with an evening programme of non-Western music, theatre and dance from visiting performers. There is also a restaurant, the Ekeko, which serves up typically tropical snacks, lunches and evening meals. There is a separate museum for children (*see* Tropenmuseum Junior, *p82*) though there is much to interest especially the older child in the Tropenmuseum.

The museum shop stocks a range of exclusive handmade arts and crafts from the tropics and subtropics. The colourful Dappermarkt (market) is just a short walk away.

Linnaeusstraat 2. Tel: (020) 568 8215; www.tropenmuseum.nl.

Soeterijn Theatre: (020) 568 8500. Open: daily 10am–5pm. Closed: 1 Jan, 30 Apr, 5 May & 25 Dec. Admission charge. Tram: 9, 10 & 14. Bus: 22. Nearby: Zoo (Artis).

Tropenmuseum Junior (Children's Museum)

This museum is a separate branch of the Tropenmuseum (Tropical Museum, *see p80*), which mounts special exhibitions for children and an imaginative range of hands-on workshop activities. The aim is to introduce young people to different cultures and ways of life. For example, they learn about life in the Asante Kingdom in Ghana by exploring clan staffs, stools, costumes, jewellery and drums from a reconstructed Asante palace. These events are meant for children from ages 6 to 13.

Linnaeusstraat 2. Tel: (020) 568 8215. Open daily 10am–5pm. Closed 1 Jan, 30 Apr & 25 Dec. Admission charge. Tram: 9, 10 & 14 & bus 22. Nearby: Zoo (Artis).

Van Gogh Museum

From the outside the Van Gogh Museum, designed by Gerrit Rietveld and completed in 1973, is a stark and

VAN GOGH THE MISFIT

Van Gogh's artistic career lasted a mere ten years, yet he painted over 2,000 works – 200 alone in the 15 months he spent in Arles. Painting was a passion ('one works without being aware', he wrote) and he would even work all night with candles stuck around the rim of his hat.

Van Gogh sold only one painting in his life; he was so poor that his diet consisted of meagre amounts of bread and more copious amounts of coffee and alcohol. Chronic undernourishment and lack of sleep may have contributed to his mental breakdown. In a famous quarrel he threatened his friend Gauguin with a knife and then, in a fit of remorse, severely cut his own ear. He admitted himself to an asylum, but not long afterwards, aged 37, he shot himself.

Only after his death were his talents appreciated, and his works now command world-record auction prices.

unwelcoming building. Inside, the huge whitewashed walls glow with the intense colours of Van Gogh's canvases. The collection, comprising some 200 paintings and over 500 drawings, was bequeathed to the city of Amsterdam by Van Gogh's nephew, also called Vincent. A selection of this work is displayed on the first floor – on the ground floor is the permanent collection of 19th-century art. The rest of the museum (including the spectacular new wing, designed by Kisho Kurokawa and opened in 2000) is used for excellent temporary exhibitions that throw light on Van Gogh's achievement by comparing it with the work of his friends and contemporaries.

Van Gogh's work is presented in chronological order, beginning with his early studies of peasant life. These were painted in 1884–5 when Van Gogh was living at the family rectory in Nuenen, a village in Noord Brabant province surrounded by peat moorland. The colours of the soil are reflected in these sombre sketches of coarse faces and rough hands. *The Potato Eaters*, an early masterpiece, still has an arresting force, though Van Gogh explained, in a letter to his brother Theo, that he did not intend to present rural life as brutalised and backward; 'I have tried to make it clear,' he wrote, 'that those people, eating their potatoes in the lamplight, have dug the earth with those very hands they put in the dish, and so it speaks of manual labour, and how they have honestly earned their food.'

The next section covers Van Gogh's time in Paris (1886–8) and his various experiments with *pointillisme* and the light, airy style of the Impressionists. The next section, covering his period in Arles (1888–9) shows a sudden transformation in his work. The paintings of this period are vivid and intense, the colours stunning – the blazing *Sunflowers*, the brilliant white of peach blossom against a turquoise sky, the blues and yellows of harvest

(*continued on p90*)

Amsterdam

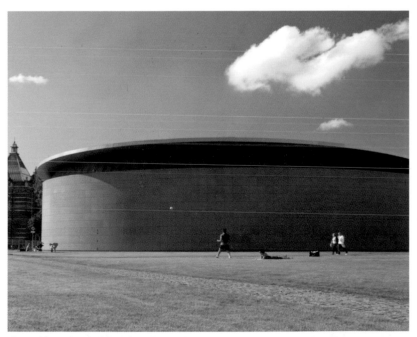

The starkly modern building of the Van Gogh Museum

Touring the Eastern Harbour

In the past ten years, the Oostelijk Havengebied (Eastern Harbour) area between Centraal Station and Zeeburg Island has experienced an inspired renaissance, as well as evolving into an architectural beauty spot. Four peninsulas, or 'islands', to the east (KNSM, Java, Borneo and Sporenburg) have been developed as residential developments in an area known as 'the new Venice'. This area was created between 1876 and 1927 because Amsterdam's oldest harbour, the IJ, was no longer accessible due to the construction of Centraal Station. These man-made 'islands' became the heart of Amsterdam's harbour until after 1950 when they were no longer big enough to accommodate larger ships and the growing transport traffic, and new harbours were created to the west.

To get to the New Islands, you can take a ferry from behind Centraal Station to the tip of Java Island. From there you can walk to KNSM island and then on to Sporenburg and Borneo. There is a range of new architecture as well as innovative restoration to the former buildings. Buses 39 and 43 will also take you there from Centraal Station. Tram 26 from the Centraal Station will take you along the route as far as the

The glass exterior of the imposing Muziekgebouw

This old Ukrainian fishing boat is now a café-restaurant

newly developed IJburg area with a small beachfront.

If you walk along the newly named Piet Heinkade, which is the street running east from behind Centraal Station, you will pass the spectacular Muziekgebouw aan het 'IJ (Music Building for contemporary music and jazz) with its glass exterior and popular Star Café. Just next door is the Passengers' Terminal building, where more than 100 cruise ships arrive each year. The nearly transparent building has a design that gives an impression of breaking waves. The Post Amsterdam (street name changes to Oostelijke Handelskade) is a former warehouse that has been converted into an interior design showroom. A branch of Jamie Oliver's London restaurant *Fifteen* is located here and offers waterfront views as well as cooking from a young team of chefs trained from scratch. At No 21 is Pakhuis de Zwijger, a former cold-storage facility.

As you proceed east, you will come to the Jan Schaeferbrug (a 200m/ 656ft bridge) which connects the quay between the Passengers' Terminal and Java Island. The hip *Club Panama* (nightclub, café, restaurant, cultural centre) greets you at No 4. On the right side is a distinguished building dating to 1918, the Lloyd Hotel, which after extensive renovation was reopened in 2004. Once used as a detention centre and later an artist's studio, it now caters to an artistic crowd. On the Veemkade, in the water of the IJ harbour opposite KNSM Island, lies the ship *Odessa*, an old fishing boat from the Ukraine, which is a popular café-restaurant.

There are several cafés on KNSM island, so continue your walkabout at your leisure.

Walk: Around the Amstel

Amsterdam is named after the River Amstel which once flowed through the heart of the city. The original course has since been filled in, but on this walk visitors will see the stretch that survives, a broad rolling watercourse that brings the canal circle to an abrupt end in the east of the city.

Allow 1 hour.

Start at Muntplein. Its landmark tower, the Munttoren, was given its elegant steeple by Hendrik de Keyser in the early 17th century. Cross the chaotic junction and walk down Reguliersbreestraat to the cinema halfway down on the right.

1 Pathé Tuschinski

This Art Deco cinema stands incongruously surrounded by fast-food outlets and tacky souvenir shops. Founded by Abram Tuschinski, a Polish Jew who died at Auschwitz, it opened in 1921 and retains all its original fittings – go inside to admire the lavish carpets, murals and lamps of the foyer, and to check what films are showing. Tours are available.

Turn right out of the cinema for Rembrandtplein.

2 Rembrandtplein

A statue of Rembrandt, on the right, looks down with a bemused expression on the square that bears his name. The commercial square is completely

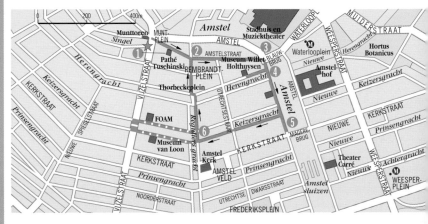

surrounded by pavement cafés.

Walk down Amstelstraat, passing the formal gardens of the Museum Willet-Holthuysen on the right, to the Amstel.

3 Amstel

Straight ahead is the unmissable bulk of the Stadhuis/Muziektheater complex, completed in 1986. Alongside is the Blauwbrug of a century earlier, modelled on the flamboyant Pont Alexandre III in Paris. This is a more restrained version with boat-shaped piers and lampstands. On the opposite bank, to the right, you will see the long façade of the Amstelhof, built in 1683 and now under the operation of Amsterdam's branch of the Hermitage museum. The new building is set to open at the end of 2008 next to the existing Hermitage complex.

Turn right and follow the Amstel embankment to the first bridge.

4 Herengracht

Look right from the bridge down this leafy canal with its patrician houses. If you have the time, walk down the right-hand embankment to visit the Museum Willet-Holthuysen, No 605, and see its stately 18th-century interiors.

Continue along the Amstel, heading for the white lifting bridge.

5 Magere Brug

The 'Skinny Bridge' is over 300 years old and derives its name from an earlier, even narrower, bridge. This has become one of the cherished landmarks of Amsterdam. On the opposite bank is the stately Koninklijk Theater Carré, built in 1887 as a circus venue, now used to stage popular musical performances.

Retrace your steps to Keizersgracht and walk down the left-hand embankment, noting the variety of gable styles represented on the buildings opposite. Cross Utrechtsestraat and continue along Keizersgracht, looking out for the huge figure of Neptune on the gable of No 695.

6 Reguliersgracht

The next crossing marks the junction of Keizersgracht and Reguliersgracht, at a photogenic spot featured on countless postcards. Five bridges span the junction and long vistas open up in every direction, each embankment lined by tipsy leaning houses.

Walkers now have a choice. Continue along the north side of Keizersgracht, and you will pass the former Fodor Museum (No 609) on the right, now the FOAM photo museum, and the palatial Museum van Loon (No 672) opposite.

Alternatively, turn right, down Reguliersgracht (named after the Regulars, or monks, who lived here until 1532), to return to Rembrandtplein.

NEARBY

Kerkstraat runs parallel to Keizersgracht to the left. On the Kerkstraat/Reguliersgracht junction there is the unusual Amstelkerk, built in 1670 in timber as a temporary measure – a bigger brick church was planned but never built.

Ethnic Amsterdam

Nearly a quarter of Amsterdam's population is of non-Dutch origin, a legacy of colonialism and of the 'guest workers' policy of the 1960s. Before World War II, the Dutch Empire spanned the globe, from the Antilles and Dutch Guyana to South Africa, and from there, via the 8,000 islands of the East Indies, to Tasmania.

In 1949, Indonesia was the first of the former colonies to secure independence, but ties between the two countries remain strong; thousands of Amsterdammers have island ancestry and their contribution to city life is most evident in the large number of excellent Indonesian restaurants.

A man of Vietnamese origin selling vegetables

Muslim women shop in a busy street

Dutch Guyana – modern Surinam – gained independence in 1975, and 150,000 Surinamese have since exercised their right to settle in the Netherlands. Another 35,000 migrants from Turkey and Morocco arrived in the 1960s, deliberately imported to do the low-paid manual jobs that the Dutch themselves were not willing to do.

Amsterdammers pride themselves on a long tradition of hospitality, but tension nevertheless exists between different parts of the community. Some white residents blame incomers for crime and complain about the cost to the city of housing, welfare and unemployment benefits. Equally, immigrants blame crime on the white population, whom they see as immoral and irreligious, and they complain that their cultures are misunderstood.

Even so, great efforts are being made to create a harmonious society. The area known as De Pijp (The Pipe) is a good example of successful integration. Most residents here are young and determined to get on.

Albert Cuypstraat, the area's colourful market (see p138), is a cheerful melting pot, an exotic bazaar catering to all tastes, and the best place to experience Amsterdam in all its ethnic diversity.

Vincent Van Gogh's *Irises* at the Van Gogh Museum

scenes and landscapes all speak of Van Gogh's enthusiasm for 'the full effect of colour'.

The two final sections of the museum show the pictures he produced while staying at the St Remy asylum (1889–90), after the famous ear-cutting incident, and in the last weeks of his life when he stayed at Auvers before committing suicide. These paintings fluctuate between tortured abstract depictions of twisted tree roots and flashes of Van Gogh at his most accomplished – *Irises*, for example, was dashed off in a moment of inspiration between the bouts of depression that finally brought the brief life of this visionary artist to an end.
Paulus Potterstraat 7. Tel: (020) 570 5200; www.vangoghmuseum.nl. Open: daily 10am–6pm (10pm Fri). Closed: 1 Jan. Admission charge. Tram: 2 & 5. Nearby: Rijksmuseum, Stedelijk Museum.

Museum Van Loon

The atmospheric Museum Van Loon was designed in 1672 by Adriaan Dortsman and has the figures of Minerva, Mars, Vulcan and Ceres on the cornice. One of the first owners of the house was Ferdinand Bol, a pupil of Rembrandt, who married a rich wife and promptly gave up painting. Another was Catharina Trip, whose initials, along with those of her husband, Abraham van Hagen, are carved into the staircase balustrade. The house was purchased in 1884 by Hendrik van Loon and it now features a near-complete sequence of Van Loon family portraits, from 17th-century paintings to 20th-century photographs. The period furnishings all have the patina that comes from time and use, creating a mood of faded grandeur.
Keizersgracht 672. Tel: (020) 624 5255; www.museumvanloon.nl. Open: Wed–Mon 11am–5pm. Admission charge. Tram: 16, 24 & 25. Nearby: Museum Willet-Holthuysen.

Verzetsmuseum (Dutch Resistance Museum)

The Dutch Resistance Museum is housed in a former synagogue in the wealthy Plantage suburb where Anne Frank and her family lived until they went into hiding. The displays recall the many ingenious ways that the Dutch Resistance sought to sabotage the Nazi occupation.

The exhibits include a bicycle-powered printing press used for forging documents to help Jews escape arrest and for producing underground newspapers such as *Het Parool* (The Password), which continues to circulate in Amsterdam to this day.

There is a reconstruction of a hiding place used by *onderduikers*, 'divers', along with contemporary photographs, video material and radio broadcasts, all of which help to bring this fascinating subject vividly to life.

Plantage Kerklaan 61. Tel: (020) 620 2535; www.verzetsmuseum.org. Open: Tue–Fri 10am–5pm, Mon, Sat–Sun & public holidays noon–5pm. Closed: 1 Jan, 30 Apr & 25 Dec. Admission charge. Tram: 9, 10 & 14.

Museum Willet-Holthuysen

Of the several Golden Age houses open to the public in Amsterdam, this is the grandest. The imposing mansion was built in 1689 and left to the city in 1895 along with a large collection of glass, Delftware, clocks, furniture and silver.

At first, nobody wanted to see a house full of 'Victorian' furniture little different to what many Amsterdammers had in their own home. The bored curator spent his time writing a scurrilous novel about the former owners and it was jokingly said that the museum was an ideal place for clandestine lovers to meet without being observed.

Visitors now come in large numbers, enjoying a glimpse below stairs of the 18th-century kitchen stacked with gleaming copper pans, before exploring the grander rooms upstairs with their ceiling paintings, Aubusson tapestries and gilded chandeliers.

Herengracht 605. Tel: (020) 523 1822; www.museumwillet-holthuysen.nl. Open: Mon–Fri 10am–5pm, Sat–Sun & public holidays 11am–5pm. Closed: 1 Jan, 30 Apr & 25 Dec. Admission charge. Tram: 4, 9 & 14.

The imposing façade of the Museum Willet-Holthuysen

Walk: unknown Amsterdam: The Western Islands

If you have fallen in love with Amsterdam and want to buy a bijou city residence, you could do worse than head for the three man-made islands located in the western harbour. The three islands are Prinseneiland, Realeneiland and Bickerseiland, collectively known as the Westelijke Eilanden (Western Islands). They were constructed in the 1630s, originally to store hazardous and inflammable materials well away from the residential heart of the city.

The stately 17th-century warehouses survive, with their huge sail-shaped window shutters. Most have already been turned into apartments, while others are in the process of being converted. Unconverted warehouses are much in demand by artists, sculptors and photographers because of their huge floor area and bohemian ambience. Unfortunately they have become largely unaffordable and are increasingly being transformed into luxury living spaces where the wealthy can retire.

The Western Islands have a distinctive 'village' atmosphere, enhanced by the lack of traffic. Herons perch on the ancient lifting bridges that link the islands, all as attractive and as well preserved as the more famous Magere Brug in the city centre. Swans, moorhens and ducks nest on the canal banks where old sailing ships and houseboats are moored alongside tugs, barges and wrecked hulls – their owners intending, optimistically, to restore them one day. *The best way to reach the islands from*

Amsterdam Centraal Station is to walk down Haarlemmerstraat and Haarlemmerdijk, the latter a characterful street lined by a mix of inexpensive neighbourhood shops and cafés, unique boutiques and food emporiums.

This is the 'real' Amsterdam where ordinary residents shop and pass the time of day. Alas, it has been discovered by tourists in recent years and has become a bit too popular. The street ends at Haarlemmerplein where a ponderous triumphal arch, built in the 19th century as a monumental entrance to the city from Haarlem, now stands unloved on a busy traffic island. *Turn right, crossing the busy road, then pass under the railway viaduct.*

Suddenly you are in a different world. Take the first bridge on the right and you will reach Bickerseiland. Continue straight through and you will hear the sounds of hens and goats as you turn left on Bickersgracht; the source is the

Kinderboerderij (children's farm) **de Dierencapel** just round the bend (*open: daylight hours; free admission, but donations welcome*).

Carry on to the right and cross the bridge to Realeneiland and you will reach Zandhoek where there is a fine row of 17th-century houses with spout, step and bell gables. Plaques on the house fronts depict Noah's Ark, St Peter and St John, anchors, boats and a white horse. The last in the row, No 15, is a restaurant, De Gouden Reael, renowned for its regional French cuisine (*see p163*). Opposite, you will see sailing barges moored in Westerdok.

Beyond this point the scene becomes more bleak. A lot of warehouses on Van Diemenstraat have been turned into enterprise buildings, and one, No 410, is now the Veem (Warehouse) Theatre where dance and mime are performed. Otherwise the empty warehouses are now being converted under the IJ-Oever Project, a hugely ambitious regeneration plan designed to provide yet more conference centres, marinas, parks and museums as well as homes for 20,000 families and office premises designed for multinational companies. *Walk all the way back to Bickersgracht and cross the canal (to the left), and you will arrive on Prinseneiland.*

Many plastic artists have their studios here; there are also two galleries, one at No 439, Maria Chailloux, and one at No 14A, Ans Markus. Dutch buyers are more fortunate than foreign visitors – they can take out an interest-free loan from the government to buy the works on display, repaying in instalments. The idea is to encourage people of ordinary means to buy art.

Continue and soon you will emerge beneath the railway viaduct again; cross the road, walk straight on and you will find yourself back in Haarlemmerdijk.

Unknown Amsterdam: The Western Islands

Restored 17th-century apartments in Zandhoek

Gable types

Amsterdam has been described as a city of 'architectural good manners', a city of few ostentatious buildings but of a myriad charming details. Seventeenth-century planning laws ensured that all houses were built of brick or stone to standard widths, so that canalside homeowners had limited scope for placing their personal stamp on the property.

Still, to stand out, they varied the number and size of windows in the façade; huge expanses of gleaming glass advertised the wealth of the owner, since glass was an expensive commodity. Another way of expressing individualism was to cover the crown and sides of the gable with sculptures or ornamental frills and flourishes.

Gables were originally very plain. They were designed to disguise the roof ridge, built at right angles to the canal. The earliest type was the point gable, a simple inverted 'V' that precisely followed the shape of the roof timbers.

Next came the spout gable which is the same as a point gable except with a chimney-like rectangular protusion from the point; these two types are commonly seen on the earliest surviving warehouses. By 1600, the more ornate step gable was in use for domestic buildings and it remained in vogue until Philip Vingboons designed the first neck gable, shaped like the shoulders and neck of a wine bottle, for the

Look up and feast your eyes on gable art

In the face of architectural conformity gables express Amsterdam's individuality

Cromhouthuisen (now the Bijbels Museum) in 1638. This quickly became fashionable, and was joined by the bell gable in 1660.

From 1670, the owners of grand houses on the Golden Bend of the canal circle began to reject the traditional Dutch style. Sandstone was used for the façades instead of brick, and the frontages were now too wide to be spanned by a single gable.

Instead the roof line was hidden by pediments, balustrades and cornices, often embellished with Baroque swags and garlands or neoclassical sculpture.

However, right up to the last century, the gable remained in use for humbler homes, and a short stroll along the canal circle reveals just how well these simple geometric shapes lend themselves to an infinite number of variations.

Walk: Nieuwmarkt and the University Quarter

This walk covers some important but little-visited architectural monuments in the south of the old city.

Allow 1½ hours.

Start at Dam Square and walk to the right of the Nationaal Monument, down Damstraat. Continue into Oude Hoogstraat.

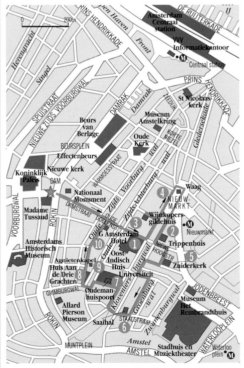

1 Oost-Indisch Huis

A low arch beside No 24 leads into the courtyard of East India House, once the headquarters of the powerful trading company.

Return to Oude Hoogstraat, turning right, then left on to Kloveniersburgwal.

2 Trippenhuis

On the opposite bank is the palatial Trippenhuis, built between 1660 and 1664 by Justus Vingboons. The interior (not open to the public) housed the Rijksmuseum collection during most of the 19th century.

Take the next turning left, Koestraat.

3 Wijnkopersgildehuis

Halfway down, at No 10, is the former headquarters of the wine importers' guild. The frieze above the door depicts St Urban among grape vines.

*Return to Kloveniersburgwal and turn
left up to Nieuwmarkt.*

4 Nieuwmarkt

The dominant building is the Waag
(Weighhouse), originally built in 1488 as
a gate in the city wall. The octagonal
tower in the centre, added in 1690,
served as the lecture theatre of the
Surgeons' Guild (as depicted in
Rembrandt's *The Anatomy Lecture
of Dr Jan Deyman*). The Waag now
houses changing exhibitions and
a restaurant.
*Walk down the opposite bank of
Kloveniersburgwal for a closer look at the
Trippenhuis. Note the two doors, one for
each of the Trip brothers for whom it was
built; behind the unified façade there
were two separate residences. Turn left in
Nieuwe Hoogstraat and first right in
Zanddwarsstraat.*

5 Zuiderkerk

Straight ahead is the tower of
Zuiderkerk (South Church). The
church, designed in 1603, was the first
in the city built for Calvinist worship.
*Walk to Raamgracht and, after walking
three sides of a square, continue down
Groenburgwal, turning right at the
timber lifting bridge.*

6 Staalstraat

This short but picturesque street is
lined with up-market shops. The
Saaihal (Serge Hall), No 7, was built in
1614 by Pieter de Keyser.
Cross the iron lifting bridge, turn right

*on Kloveniersburgwal and look for a gate
on the left just after No 82.*

7 Oudemanhuispoort

Above the 'Gate of the Old Men's
Home', sculptures show Charity
between two beggars. On the right is
the former old people's home, built in
1786, now part of the university.
*Walk through the passage where there are
stalls of antiquarian books for sale.*

8 Huis aan de Drie Grachten

Facing you as you emerge is the
delightful 'House on the Three Canals',
built in 1609, and so-called because it
has three step-gabled façades, each
looking out on to a different canal.
*Walk past the house and turn right up
OZ Voorburgwal.*

9 Agnietenkapel

This former chapel, at No 231, was the
first home of the Atheneum Illustre, a
learned society and forerunner of the
University of Amsterdam.
*Further up on the right, look for No 197,
an Art Deco brick gateway.*

10 Grand Amsterdam Hotel

Through the gateway to the right is the
Grand Amsterdam hotel, the former
Town Hall, built in 1647 as the
Admiralty headquarters. It became the
Town Hall in 1808 when Louis
Napoleon turned the original Stadhuis,
on Dam Square, into his royal palace.
*Take the next turn left, Oude
Doelenstraat, to return to Dam Square.*

Walk: Nieumarkt and the University Quarter

Amsterdam environs

Travel within the Netherlands is extremely easy, thanks to an excellent integrated public transport system. Many of the sites covered in this section are accessible by fast, cheap and reliable Intercity trains which depart from Amsterdam Centraal Station every 15 or 30 minutes. Journey times are short: Schiphol airport and Haarlem are only 13 minutes away, Utrecht 28 minutes, Den Haag (The Hague) 35 minutes and Rotterdam an hour. Amsterdam, therefore, makes a perfect base for exploring the wider attractions of the Netherlands. All-inclusive day-trip tickets (Rail Idee, or 'Rail Idea') offer the cheapest way to travel; they include the cost of the rail fare and admission at a discount to almost all attractions. The Rail Idee can be purchased separately if you already have a valid entrance ticket or pass.

Alternatively, you can buy a one-day travel pass which allows unlimited use of the transport network. Details of both are given in the useful *Exploring Holland by Train* booklet which is available from the information centre in Amsterdam Centraal Station or before you go from the Netherlands Board of Tourism offices.

Harbour view of Rotterdam, chief port of the Netherlands

Amsterdam environs

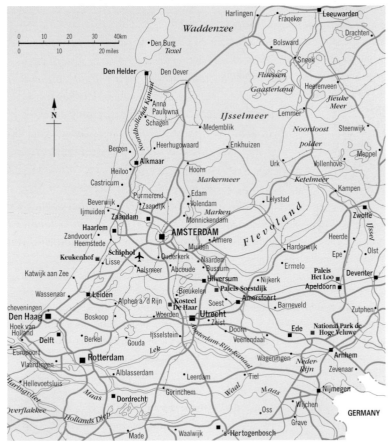

Some destinations close to Amsterdam are not on the rail network but are easily reached by buses that go from the main terminus outside Amsterdam Centraal Station, or the suburban station, Amsterdam Amstel.

If you prefer to have everything organised for you, there are numerous coach tours covering the same destination. These can be booked in person at the VVV Informatiekantoor (Tourist Information Office) at Stationsplein 10, in Amsterdam. Once you arrive at your destination you can obtain free maps and leaflets from the excellent VVV Tourist Information Offices which are usually located on the main square or near the station. You can also hire a bike for the day at most stations by presenting some form of identification and paying a small deposit.

Aalsmeer

The Aalsmeer Flower Auction
(Verenigde Bloemenveiling Aalsmeer,
or VBA) is the biggest commercial
flower market in the world. It is well
worth visiting if you are fond of plants
or just enjoy the bustle of a busy
commercial market. You do have to be
an early riser, however, to catch the
action: the auctions are at their busiest
around 9am, especially on Mondays.

Visitors watch the proceedings from
an elevated gallery which provides a
bird's-eye view of the auction itself and
all the sorting and despatch work that
goes on behind the scenes. Recorded
commentaries, in seven languages,
explain what is going on.

The VBA, founded in 1968, is a cooperative venture with a membership
of 5,000 growers who sell their pot
plants and cut flowers at Aalsmeer,
paying a commission of 5 per cent of
sales to fund the operation. Sales are
conducted using the 'Dutch auction'
system. This works in a way that is the
opposite of normal auction procedure,
with prices starting at the top and
coming down until a buyer is found.
Prices are indicated by a huge clock
above the auctioneer's head marked out
in divisions from 100 down to 1. The
clock pointer starts at 100 – the highest
price – and sweeps downwards until a
buyer, seated at a computerised desk,
presses a button to stop the clock at the
price he or she is prepared to pay.

Computerisation is the key to the
speed and efficiency of the whole

An auction of colours at Aalsmeer

operation. Invoices and dispatch
information are prepared automatically
as soon as the 'buy' button is pressed.
The computer also handles all the
currency calculations – more than
80 per cent of the produce sold here
is exported.

Some 10,000 transactions an hour
are conducted in this way in five
separate auction rooms devoted to
different types of plants. The lots are
delivered to the buyer within 15
minutes of the sale; around 350 buyers
rent packing space on the premises, and
some 2,000 trucks, laden with sweet-
smelling produce, leave the building
daily for all parts of Europe.

The market is huge; with an area
equivalent to 100 football pitches
(715,000sq m/177 acres), it is said to be
the biggest commercial building in the
world. Market staff use bicycles to get
around. Aalsmeer is big business in

every way; the Netherlands is the world's leading producer of pot plants and flowers, with 51 per cent of the market, and much of that produce passes through here.

On the lighter side: once a year, on the first Saturday of September, everyone involved in the market – growers, buyers and florists – stages a huge and colourful parade of imaginatively decorated cars and trucks smothered by a massive tapestry of flowers, from Aalsmeer to the centre of Amsterdam.

12km (7 miles) southwest of Amsterdam at Legmeerdijk 313, Aalsmeer.
Tel: (0297) 392 185. Getting there: bus 172 from Amsterdam Centraal Station.
Open: Mon–Fri 7.30–11am.
Admission charge.

Alkmaar

Alkmaar is famed for the traditional cheese market held in the main square every Friday morning in summer months. White-garbed porters in straw hats (red, green, blue or yellow, denoting the particular group to which they belong) carry the huge rounds of yellow-waxed cheese on wooden sledges across the square into the Renaissance **Waaggebouw** (Weigh House) where the actual selling takes place. The streets around the square are crammed with stalls selling antiques, crafts and – of course – local cheese. Barrel organs and buskers add to the festive atmosphere. The town itself has several fine buildings: the 15th-century **Grote Kerk** (Great Church), the **Stadhuis** (Town Hall) of 1520 and the Waaggebouw of 1582 (housing a cheese museum) can all be visited. The **Stedelijk Museum** has an interesting collection of antique toys.

37km (23 miles) northwest of Amsterdam. Getting there: train line 1 to Den Helder. Journey time 32 minutes.
Tourist information: Waagplein 2–3. Tel: (072) 511 4284; www.vvvweb.nl. Cheese market open: mid-Apr–mid-Sept, Fri 10am–12.30pm.

Say cheese at Alkmaar

Windmills at the open-air Arnhem Museum

Arnhem

The name of Arnhem will always be associated with Operation Market Garden, the heroic but disastrous World War II battle which was immortalised in the film, *A Bridge Too Far*. The battle was an ambitious attempt to end the war in time for Christmas 1944. The military leaders involved, Field Marshal Montgomery and General Eisenhower, planned to invade Germany after capturing the strategic Rhine bridge at Arnhem. This involved flying troops into the heart of the Netherlands, still under Nazi occupation. General Browning, in charge of the Airborne Divisions, had misgivings about the operation, and it was he who told Montgomery, 'We might be going a bridge too far'.

He was right; when 35,000 troops were parachuted into Arnhem on 17 September 1944 they found the bridges heavily defended by the tanks and artillery of the 2nd SS Panzer Division. Some 600 Allied troops fought their way to Arnhem bridge and defended it for four days before being forced to

withdraw. The battle ended with defeat for the Allies and the death of thousands of soldiers.

Visitors can visit the battle sites and trace the course of events, by means of models and an audio-visual presentation, at the **Airborne Museum** in Oosterbeek, 8km (5 miles) west of Arnhem. Nearby, on the north bank of the Rhine, in Oosterbeek is the **Airborne War Cemetery**, beautifully maintained by the War Graves Commission.

Arnhem has two other outstanding attractions. On the outskirts of the town is the **Nederlands Openlucht** (Open-Air) **Museum** where 80 traditional buildings have been rescued from their original sites and reconstructed. These include windmills, farmhouses, schools, factories, shops, churches and inns dating from the 17th century. The interiors are used to display traditional costumes, folk art, furniture and tools, and there are regular craft demonstrations.

Some 6km (4 miles) to the north of Arnhem is the **Nationaal Park Hoge Veluwe**, a huge tract of forest and heath. Free bikes provide the means of getting around, and the main highlight is the **Kröller-Müller Museum**, at the centre of the park, where over 200 works by Van Gogh are displayed, together with works by Picasso, Braque and many modern artists. In the sculpture garden around the museum, works by Moore, Rodin, Hepworth and others are all the more entrancing for their background of trees, water and open skies.

72km (45 miles) southeast of Amsterdam. Getting there: train lines 4 & 5 to Nijmegen; journey time 75 minutes; change at Arnhem for Oosterbeek, journey time 4 minutes. Bus 3 (to Alteveer) goes from Arnhem station to the Openluchtmuseum, and bus 107 (to Harderwijk) goes to the Park Hoge Veluwe; in summer a special museum bus, No 12, serves both museums. Tourist information: Stationsplein 45. Tel: (0900) 202 4075.

Airborne Museum open: Mon–Sat 10am–5pm, Sun & public holidays noon–5pm. Openlucht Museum open: mid-Apr–Oct, daily 10am–5pm. Admission charge. Hoge Veluwe Park visitors' centre open: daily 8am–sunset. Kröller-Müller Museum open: Tue–Sat 10am–5pm (sculpture garden closes 4.30pm).

Aviodrome
(National Aviation Theme Park)

A short train ride from Schiphol is Lelystad, where you can find the Dutch National Aviation Theme Park and Museum. It is popular with children, who are allowed to climb into the cockpit of one of the aircraft. The dome-shaped building shelters various historic aircraft, ranging from the Wright Flyer of 1903 to a Mercury space capsule. It also celebrates the Dutch contribution to aviation history; the Dutch national carrier, KLM, was the world's first commercial airline,

flying locally built Fokker FVII aircraft from 1919. Posters and KLM memorabilia of the 1920s evoke the romance of flight in those early days. In the 'top down' exhibit, one can have a simulated experience of riding in an air balloon over interesting sites in the Netherlands.

There is a sober reminder of the aerial warfare of World War II in the salvaged remains of a British bomber, and plenty of diversions in the form of films, slide shows and an exhibition on the importance of Schiphol airport to the Dutch economy.

Pelikaan 50, Lelystad Airport. Getting there: train to Schiphol station then train from platform 2 for Lelystad. Take bus 148 to Lelystad Airport, from where the Aviodrome is signposted. Tel: (320) 289 840; www.aviodome.nl. Open: Tue–Sun 10am–5pm and Mon during school holidays. Closed: 1 Jan. Admission charge. Open later in summer for special events.

The Aviodrome is popular with visitors of all ages

Delft

Delft has given its name to the distinctive blue-and-white pottery that has been produced here since the 17th century when Dutch East India Company ships first started bringing back delicate porcelain wares from China. The potters of the region immediately began to copy these wares but decorated their plates, jugs, tiles and tulip jars with scenes from everyday life, biblical subjects and Dutch landscapes. The industry nearly collapsed in the 19th century in the face of competition from England. The only firm to survive in Delft was **De Porceleyne Fles**, founded in 1653 and still going strong. If you want to know more you should head straight for this company's Visitor Centre, which exhibits typical products and offers factory tours throughout the day.

There is, though, far more to Delft than pottery. On the main square, Markt, you will find the Renaissance **Stadhuis** (Town Hall) built in 1618 by Hendrik de Keyser. The statue in the centre of the square commemorates the lawyer Hugo Grotius, born in Delft in 1583, whose great work on the conduct of war laid the foundations for modern international law.

Opposite, **Nieuwe Kerk**, with its soaring 15th-century choir, contains the mausoleum of William of Orange, leader of the Dutch revolt against Spanish rule and the father of the Netherlands. The monument, another work by Hendrik de Keyser, was designed in 1614; in allegorical form, it depicts the ideals on which the newly independent Dutch Republic was based – liberty, justice, religion and fortitude.

William of Orange met an untimely end in Delft in 1584; he was assassinated in the nearby convent of St Agatha, now the **Prinsenhof Museum**, which William used as his campaign headquarters during the war against Spain. The bullet holes made by his assassin (Balthazar Gerards, a fanatical Catholic and a supporter of Spanish rule) can be seen behind glass in room 8, the Moordzaal (Murder Hall).

Apart from this morbid memorial, the rest of the museum is a delight. The traceried Gothic windows of the 15th-

The 15th-century Nieuwe Kerk in Delft

Tempting displays of Delft porcelain

century convent look out on to attractive courtyard gardens, and the walls are hung with paintings by artists of the Delft School.

Opposite the museum is the 14th-century **Oude Kerk**, with its leaning tower and beautiful 16th-century transept, built in the style known, appropriately, as Flamboyant Gothic. Inside there are the tombs of Vermeer and the Delft-born inventor of the microscope, Antonie van Leeuwenhoek, along with memorials to the Admirals Piet Hein and Maarten Tromp; the latter's tomb is carved with a realistic battle scene praised by Samuel Pepys as 'a sea-fight cut in marble, the smoke the best expressed that ever I saw'.

From the church it is worth walking the length of Oude Delft, a leafy canal lined by elegant houses. At No 199, the best collection of antique Delftware in the city can be found, housed in the **Museum Lambert van Meerten**; the interior is covered in tiles, ranging from large-scale battle scenes to cheerful depictions of children's games.

At the opposite end of Oude Delft, the courtyard houses at No 39 once served as an office of the VOC (Verenigde Oostindische Companie, better known as the Dutch East India Company). Opposite the huge former arsenal, the Armamentarium, is now the **Nederlands Legermuseum** (Dutch Army Museum).

58km (36 miles) southwest of Amsterdam. Rotterdam CS. Getting there: train journey time 55 minutes. Tourist information: Hippolytusbuurt 4. Tel: (0900) 515 1555; www.delft.nl

DELFT

De Koninklijke Porceleyne Fles
Rotterdamseweg 196. Tel: (015) 251 2030; www.royaldelft.com. Open: Mon–Sat 9am–5pm, Apr–Oct also Sun 9am–5pm. Admission charge.

Museum Lambert van Meerten
Oude Delft 199. Tel: (015) 260 2199. Open: Tue–Sat 10am–5pm, Sun & public holidays 1–5pm. Admission charge.

Nederlands Legermuseum
Korte Geer 1. Tel: (015) 215 0500; www.legermuseum.nl. Open: Tue–Fri 10am–5pm, Sat–Sun noon–5pm. Admission charge.

Nieuwe Kerk
Markt. Tel: (015) 212 3025. Open: Apr–Oct, Mon–Sat 9am–6pm; Nov–Mar, Mon–Sat 11am–4pm. Admission charge.

Oude Kerk
Oude Delft. Tel: (015) 212 3015. Open: Mon–Fri 9am–6pm, Sat 10am–5pm. Admission charge.

Museum het Prinsenhof
St Agathaplein 1. Tel: (015) 260 2358. Open: Tue–Sat 10am–5pm, Sun & public holidays 1–5pm. Admission charge.

Edam

Edam competes with Gouda for the title of cheese capital of the Netherlands; in terms of quantity of output Edam wins but, in contrast to Gouda, Edam has not turned its cheese industry into a major tourist attraction. Instead, the town is noted for the quiet calm of its numerous waterways and wooden bridges, though visitors can buy the familiar round balls of soft cheese, wrapped in a protective skin of red or yellow wax, at the ancient **Kaasmarkt** (Cheese Market) on Waagplein, built in 1592.

Edam, where the local cheese is on offer

The delightful **Edams Museum** on Damplein occupies a late Gothic house of 1530 whose small dark rooms, ladder-like stairs and hidden cupboard beds are reminiscent of life on board a ship. The building even has a curious floating cellar which sways as you walk across the floor – built, according to the local story, by a retired ship's captain who was nostalgic for the feel of the sea. Equally eccentric are the museum's portraits of three local characters, one extremely fat, another very tall and the third, Pieter Langebaard, who had, true to his name, a very long beard which he showed off as he toured the Netherlands to raise funds for the local orphanage. The town's other important monument is the **Grote Kerk** (Great Church), rebuilt after a fire in 1602 and notable for its stained glass depicting historical scenes. Several operators offer boat tours in summer to neighbouring towns around the former Zuider Zee.

22km (14 miles) north of Amsterdam. Getting there: bus 112, 114 & 116 from Amsterdam Centraal Station; journey time 35 minutes.
Tourist information: Damplein 1. Tel: (0299) 315 125; www.vvv-edam.nl. Kaasmarkt open: July–Aug, Wed 10.30am–12.30pm. Edams Museum: Damplein 8. Tel: (0299) 372 431. Open: Easter–autumn half-term school holiday, Tue–Sat 10am–4.30pm, Sun 1.30–4.30pm. Admission charge.

Enkhuizen

The fascinating story of the reclamation of the Zuiderzee and of the vanished way of life of its former fishing villages is told at the **Zuiderzeemuseum** in Enkhuizen. Drainage of the Zuider Zee began as early as the 17th century with the creation of the Beemster, Purmer and Wormer polders. Dykes were built to hold back the sea, and drainage canals were dug; windmills, fitted with scoop wheels, were then used to raise the water high enough to flow back into the sea. The land thus reclaimed was very fertile; villages surrounding the Zuiderzee became wealthy on the profits from arable crops, adding to their income from marine trade and fishing, and they built imposing town halls to celebrate their new prosperity.

By the mid-18th century, the sea had silted up to the extent that big ships could no longer reach Amsterdam, a problem resolved by digging the Noordzee Kanaal, which opened in 1876. The widespread use of steam pumps from the mid-19th century added impetus to land reclamation, but the new fields were always liable to flooding from the combined forces of high tides and heavy rainfall. After a devastating flood that occurred in 1916, a long-standing plan to dam the Zuiderzee, first mooted by the engineer Cornelis Lely in 1891, was revived. The Afsluitdijk (Enclosing Dyke) was built by sinking woven willow mattresses to act as a raft, thus preventing the huge weight of stones and concrete piled on top from sinking into the sea bed. When the dyke was completed in 1932, flags flew at half mast in the port towns round the shore, which were now cut off from the sea.

The old tidal Zuiderzee became a shallow inland lake and was rechristened the IJsselmeer. By subdividing the lake with further dams, huge areas of marshland were drained and seeded with grass to draw off the salt before being turned over to agriculture. In this way the new province of Flevoland was created, and its capital, named Lelystad after the 19th-century engineer, received its first settlers in 1967.

Enkhuizen was one of the ports to suffer from an abrupt end to its former way of life; it had once been the foremost herring port in the Netherlands. As compensation for the loss of income, it was chosen as the site for the splendid Zuiderzeemuseum (Wierdijk) – two museums, in fact, consisting of the indoor **Binnenmuseum**, opened in 1950, and the open-air Buitenmuseum, opened in 1983.

The Binnenmuseum is located in a splendid Renaissance building built on the waterfront in 1625 and known as the Peperhuis because, under Dutch East India Company ownership, it had been used for storing pepper imported from Indonesia. Room 1 of the museum houses a collection of historic Zuiderzee fishing boats, rooms 4 to 7 are devoted to locally made furniture and rooms 13 to 15 to traditional costume. It is clear from the exhibits that each village developed its own distinctive style, not just in dress but even in shipbuilding techniques, a reflection of the fact that these villages, though only a few kilometres apart, were rivals for trade and emphasised their differences in numerous ways.

The open-air museum is, appropriately enough, reached by boat which passes among the traditional sailing craft moored in the harbour. The museum consists of more than 130 buildings reconstructed to form complete streets modelled on the towns from which they were rescued; thus you can walk from Monnickendam to Edam, from Edam to Amsterdam, and from the city to the more rural village of Staveren in the course of a few hours. Informative labelling explains the history of each building and its former occupants. Many are furnished in period style or used to demonstrate crafts, such as baking, herring curing, tanning and rope making.
If the museums do not keep you occupied for a whole day, you can always take a boat trip from the harbour (summer only) to **Medemblik**, with its steam train museum, which offers a steam train service to Hoorn, and 13th-century castle, or to **Urk**, with its Visserijmuseum (Fishing Museum) and excellent fish restaurants.
64km (40 miles) northeast of Amsterdam. Getting there: train from Amsterdam Centraal Station to Enkhuizen. Journey time 60 minutes.

Tourist information: Tussen Twee Havens. Tel: (0228) 313 164; www.vvweb.nl.
Zuiderzeemuseum: Wierdijk 12–22. Tel: (0228) 351 135; www.zuiderzeemuseum.nl.
Daily 10am–5pm from 1 Jan–30 Mar & 29 Oct–31 Dec. Closed Mon and 1 Jan, 25 Dec. Museum park is open as walking park 29 Oct–30 Mar.

Gouda

For those interested in the traditional cheese market, Gouda should be visited on Thursday mornings in summer. Here white-coated experts handle and sample the cheese with all the respect usually reserved for the finest wines. Gouda develops different characteristics as it ages and several types are sold: *jong* (young) is creamy and mild,

Fishers' Monument, Urk

The stained-glass window at Gouda is part of a series of windows at St Janskerk

series of windows given by various donors when the church was rebuilt after a fire in 1522. Local guilds were among the sponsors and they chose appropriate biblical themes – *Jonah and the Whale* for the fishmongers, *Balaam and his Ass* for the butchers. Philip II of Spain donated *The Last Supper* and he is depicted with his wife, Queen Mary I of England. William the Silent, who was shortly to lead the Dutch revolt against Philip II's rule, donated *Christ Driving the Money Changers from the Temple.*

Opposite the church is the **Catharina Gasthuis**, founded as a hospice for travellers in the 14th century, now housing a fine collection of medieval art and Impressionist paintings by members of The Hague School. The town's other museum, **De Moriaan** (The Moor), is a beautifully preserved 17th-century tobacco shop displaying a collection of clay pipes, located on the former harbour at Westhaven 29.
52km (32 miles) south of Amsterdam. Getting there: train to Utrecht then change for train to Rotterdam CS/Don Haeg CS. Journey time 50 minutes. Tourist information: Markt 27. Tel: (0900) 4683 2888; www.vvvgouda.nl. Cheese market open: mid-June–mid-Aug, Thur 10am–12.30pm. Stadhuis open: Mon–Fri 9am–noon & 2–4pm, Sat 11am–3pm. St Janskerk open: Apr–Oct, Mon–Sat 9am–5pm; Nov–Mar, Mon–Sat 10am–4pm. Catharina Gasthuis open: Mon–Sat 10am–5pm, Sun noon–5pm. De Moriaan open: same as Catharina Gasthuis.

belegen is firmer and has matured for four months, *oud* (old) is ten months old and *overjarig*, the most expensive, is at least a year old, and should be pungent and crumbly. In addition there are cumin- (*komijn*) and clove- (*kruidnagel*) flavoured varieties.

The market takes place against the backdrop of the fine Flemish-style Stadhuis, built in 1450 and decorated with statues of Burgundian counts and countesses, a reminder that this part of the Netherlands was under Burgundian rule in the 15th century.

The medieval quarter, with its quiet cobbled lanes, lies to the south of the Markt. St Janskerk has the best stained glass in the Netherlands, a magnificent

Mauritshuis Museum at Den Haag

Den Haag (The Hague)

After Amsterdam, Den Haag has more to offer than any other city in the Netherlands and the museums alone will occupy more than a day, so it is worth considering an overnight stay. Den Haag is an abbreviated form of the city's old name, 's Gravenhaage, meaning the Count's Hedge. This hedge surrounded the hunting lodge of the medieval Counts of Holland, later rebuilt as a castle. The town grew up around the castle and its future was assured when Den Haag became the political capital of the Netherlands in 1586, chosen because it offered a neutral meeting ground for the leaders of the seven independent provinces created under the Treaty of Utrecht after the Spanish had been driven out.

The former castle of the Counts of Holland, the 13th-century Ridderzaal, still stands at the heart of the city. It is surrounded by the buildings of the Dutch Parliament on one side and by the **Mauritshuis** on the other, a graceful building reflected in the Hof Vijver lake, all that remains of the original castle moat. The Mauritshuis museum contains several important works: Rogier van de Weyden's *Lamentation*, Rembrandt's *The Anatomy Lesson of Dr Nicolaes Tulp*, his first public commission, Vermeer's *View of Delft* and Andy Warhol's *Queen Beatrix*.

The Mauritshuis is only one of several museums surrounding the Hof Vijver; on a short stroll you can sample the popular **Museum Gevangenpoort**, once a prison and now a 'torture museum'. The **Haags Historisch Museum** (Korte Vijverberg 7) displays old paintings of the city.

If shopping appeals more than museums, head for **The Passage**, off Buitenhof, an elegant 19th-century arcade leading to the pedestrianised shopping streets around the 15th-century **Oude Kerk**. Noordeindestraat is definitely for the wealthy, with its antique dealers and expensive restaurants.

Continuing up this street, past the royal Paleis Noordeinde, you will reach the *Panorama Mesdag*, an intriguing relic of the 19th century, and a fine example of *trompe l'oeil* painting. The circular canvas, 120m (394ft) long, shows an extraordinarily realistic view of the nearby coastal resort of Scheveningen as it was in 1881. More works by Hendrik Mesdag, a leading

Impressionist painter of The Hague School, can be seen at the artist's former home, now the Museum Mesdag, at Laan van Meerdervoort 7.

Just to the north is the huge **Vredespaleis** (Peace Palace), founded after The Hague Peace Conference of 1899 and financed by the millionaire Andrew Carnegie. The aim was to provide a forum for resolving international disputes – though it did not prevent two world wars. Now it is the seat of the International Court of Justice.

Beyond this point is the best of the city's museums, the **Haags Gemeentemuseum**. This has a big collection of modern art from The Hague School to Mondrian, Delftware and historic costumes.

The **Omniversum planetarium** next door appeals to children, as does the **Madurodam** miniature town at George Maduroplein 1, on the road to Scheveningen: this is a fascinating 1:25 scale reproduction of Dutch landscape features.

Scheveningen itself, almost a suburb of Den Haag, is a breezy North Sea coastal resort. Its attractions include an imposing Empire-style hotel, called the Kurhaus, a model of Jules Verne's *Nautilus* submarine, the Holland Casino, good fish restaurants and a long stretch of clean sandy beach.
60km (37 miles) southwest of Amsterdam. Getting there: train to Den Haag HS (Hollands Spoor) station, then change for Den Haag CS (Centraal Station). Journey time 55 minutes.

Amsterdam environs

Haags Gemeentemuseum
Stadhouderslaan 41. Tel: (070) 338 1111; www.gemeentemuseum.nl. Open: Tue–Sun 11am–5pm. Admission charge.
Madurodam
George Maduroplein 1. Tel: (070) 355 3900; www.madurodam.nl. Open: daily, late Mar–June 9am–8pm, July–Aug 9am–10pm, Sept–late Mar 9am–6pm. Admission charge.
Mauritshuis
Korte Vijverberg 8. Tel: (070) 302 3456; www.mauritshuis.nl. Open: Tue–Sat 10am–5pm, Sun & public holidays 11am–5pm (also open Mon 1 Apr–1 Sept). Admission charge.
Museum Gevangenpoort
Buitenhof 33. Tel: (070) 346 0861; www.gevangenpoort.nl. Open: Tue–Fri 10am–5pm, Sat–Sun noon–5pm. Admission charge.
Museum Mesdag
Laan van Meerdervoort 7f. Tel: (070) 362 1434; www.museummesdag.nl. Open: Tue–Sun noon–5pm. Admission charge.
Omniversum
President Kennedylaan 5. Tel: (0900) 666 4837; www.omniversum.nl. Open: daily during school holidays 10am–10pm, otherwise Mon 9.30am–3pm, Tue–Wed 9.30am–5pm, Thur–Fri 9.30am–10pm, Sat–Sun 10am–10pm; planetarium performances on the hour. Admission charge.
Panorama Mesdag
Zeestraat 65. Tel: (070) 364 4544; www.mesdag.nl. Open: Mon–Sat 10am–5pm, Sun & public holidays noon–5pm. Admission charge.
Ridderzaal
Binnenhof 8A. Tel: (070) 364 6144. Open: guided tours Mon–Sat 10am–4pm. Admission charge.

Tourist information: Koningin Julianaplein 30, to the right of the station exit. Tel: (0900) 340 3505; www.denhaag.com

Royalty

Den Haag is the home of the Dutch royal family, and several operators offer 'royal tours' taking in the lovely 17th-century Huis ten Bosch (House in the Woods – not open to the public), where Queen Beatrix lives amid extensive parkland to the east of the city.

Wilhelmina Armgard Beatrix acceded to the throne following the abdication of her mother Queen Juliana. Her coronation as Queen Beatrix on 30 April 1980 caused great controversy. The planned festivities turned into a full-scale riot as protestors, objecting to the cost of the investiture and seeking to highlight the housing crisis, fought with police in Amsterdam. Since then, Queen Beatrix has worked hard to sweep away the mystique of the monarchy. Though she is the second-richest woman in Europe (after Queen Elizabeth II of Britain) she avoids ostentation, loves cycling in the countryside and has often said she would have been a social worker if she had not been Queen. Her husband, the late Prince Claus, a former West German diplomat, once suffered from depression and won praise for talking about it publicly and for giving help to others with a similar problem. By behaving like an ordinary modern family, the Dutch royals have overcome any lingering resentment about their privileged position.

Queen Beatrix also works with consummate professionalism to promote Dutch interests at home and abroad. Once asked to define her job she replied; 'The kingdom is something to be marketed, just like oranges,' a humorous, if unintentional, reference to the fact

The Royal Palace in Amsterdam

Huis ten Bosch (House in the Woods) is the residence of the Dutch royal family

that she is descended from the French House of Orange.

She has three sons, and the eldest, Prins Willem Alexander Claus George Ferdinand, born in 1967, is the first male heir to the Dutch crown in over 100 years. On 2 February 2002, Prince Willem Alexander married Máxima Zorreguieta, an Argentinian from the higher middle class, whose bearing and appearance charmed many. They have three daughters: Princesses Catharina-Amalia, Alexia and Ariane. The royal family has the respect and affection of the general public – as can be seen when the whole country joins in the annual celebrations on 30 April in honour of Koninginnedag, the Queen's official birthday.

Haarlem

Haarlem, the capital of Noord Holland province, is a mere 13 minutes from Amsterdam by train but a world away in atmosphere. Compared with the bustle of Amsterdam, Haarlem has a peaceful, almost rural, atmosphere, and it is a pleasure to wander through its quiet streets or along the banks of the River Spaarne which winds its way round the historic centre of the city.

The ornate interior of Grote Kerk

On arrival, the station itself is worth more than a passing glance; built in 1908, it is a stylish building of Art Nouveau tilework, honey-coloured woodwork and cast iron. Jansweg leads from the station to the magnificent **Grote Kerk**, begun in the 14th century and completed in the 16th. The church was a favourite subject of 17th-century painters and may already be familiar from pictures in Amsterdam's Rijksmuseum. The simple white-painted interior serves to highlight the mighty Christian Müller organ, one of the largest in the world, and its Baroque ornamentation. Mozart (aged 10), Liszt, and Saint-Saëns have all played at its keyboard and there are regular recitals during the week. Many small shops cluster around the church walls; the one on the north side was built in 1603 as the **Vishal** (Fish Market). Alongside is the city's main square, **Grote Markt**, surrounded by notable buildings: the Renaissance **Stadhuis**, the **Vleeshal** (Meat Market) of 1603 with its giant ox-head carvings, and the **Hoofdwacht** (Guardhouse) of 1650. The statue by the church is of LJ Coster to whom the Dutch attribute the invention of printing.

To the east of Grote Kerk, Damstraat leads past the **Waag** (Weighhouse) of 1598 to the River Spaarne and its pretty white bridge. Alongside is the **Teylers Museum**, founded in 1778, and preserved in its original state. The Netherlands' oldest museum, it is full of beautifully crafted scientific instruments of polished wood and brass and cases of fossils. Also on display is a collection of drawings, including works by Michelangelo, Rembrandt and Raphael.

Returning to Grote Markt, head south down Warmoesstraat, Schagchelstraat and Groot Heiligland to the city's main attraction, the **Frans Halsmuseum**. This is located in the Oude Mannenhuis, formerly a home for elderly men, built in 1608. Frans Hals was born in Antwerp but settled in Haarlem in the 1580s and, despite being one of the greatest portrait artists of his age, ended up an impoverished inmate of this same institution.

The museum has eight of the artist's large group paintings, including one of the governors of the home, painted when Frans Hals was over 80 but quite evidently still in full possession of his powers: the picture expresses something of the bitterness he must have felt as the recipient of charity from these stern-faced and reproachful burghers. Van Gogh admired the outstanding use of colour, counting no less than 27 different tones of black.

Another superbly realised picture shows the members of the Civic Guard of St Adrian at their annual banquet, flush-faced and evidently well into their cups. Their inebriated state is conveyed partly by the unflattering facial expressions but also by the way that Frans Hals has presented the ruffs, beards and ceremonial sashes at all sorts of tipsy angles – looking at the picture

too long will make your own head begin to spin. From the museum you can weave your way back to the Grote Markt through streets where time seems to have stood still and where several shops retain their original 18th- or 19th-century fittings. Kerkstraat has a particularly good concentration of antique shops leading up to the 17th-century **Nieuwekerk**. From here, either take Lange Annastraat north to see the 17th-century *hofjes* (almshouses) that line either side, or walk back up the main shopping street, Grote Houtstraat. In Grote Markt you can rest your feet at one of several popular pavement cafés, and there are more characterful shops on Kruisstraat, leading back to the station.

23km (14 miles) west of Amsterdam. Getting there: train to Hamlem/Den Haag/Zandroort; journey time 15 minutes. Tourist information: Stationsplein 1. Tel: (0900) 616 1600.

Frans Halsmuseum
Groot Heiligland 62. Tel: (023) 511 5775; www.franshalsmuseum.nl. Open: Tue–Sat 11am–5pm, Sun & public holidays noon–5pm. Closed 1 Jan & 25 Dec. Admission charge.
Grote Kerk
Oude Groenmarkt 23. Tel: (023) 553 2040. Open: Mon–Sat 10am–4pm; guided tours Sat. Free admission.
Teylers Museum
Spaarne 16. Tel: (023) 516 0960; www.teylersmuseum.nl. Open: Tue–Sat 10am–5pm, Sun & public holidays noon–5pm. Closed: Mon, 1 Jan & 25 Dec. Admission charge.

The unique charm of Hoorn

Hoorn

Hoorn was a major port until it was cut off from the sea by the damming of the Zuider Zee (IJsselmeer). Several famous mariners were born here. JP Coen, whose statue is in the main square, founded the colony of Batavia (today's Jakarta, the capital of Indonesia), Willem Schouten rounded the southern tip of the Americas in 1616 and named it Kap Hoorn (Cape Horn) after his native town, and Abel Tasman sailed from here to discover Tasmania and New Zealand.

The historic harbour quarter from where all these momentous voyages began is well preserved and lined with old warehouses. EV Lucas, the English travel writer, described the town in 1905 as 'rising from the sea like an enchanted city … its spires and harbour tower beautifully unreal'. That same view can be enjoyed in summer by taking a boat excursion into the IJsselmeer from the pier in front of the harbour tower, the Hoofdtoren, built in 1532, and given its spire in 1651.

In the town centre, the main attraction is the **Westfries Museum** (Rode Steen 1). This occupies an ornate Mannerist building of 1632, built when Hoorn was capital of the now defunct West Friesland province and decorated with the coats of arms of the region's principal towns. The interiors evoke the splendours of the Golden Age with their 17th-century furnishings, costumes, toys and reconstructed shops. Rode Steen is also the venue for a craft fair every Wednesday in July and August at which costumed stallholders demonstrate traditional crafts such as lacemaking and clog carving.

37km (23 miles) north of Amsterdam.
Getting there: train line to Enkhuizen; journey time 37 minutes.
Tourist information: Veemarkt 4.
Tel: (072) 511 4284; www.vvvweb.nl.
Westfries Museum (www.wfm.nl). Open: Mon–Fri 11am–5pm, Sat, Sun & public holidays 2–5pm (Apr–Sept, Sun noon–5pm).

Keukenhof and Lisse

Keukenhof (Stationsweg 166A) is the showcase of the Dutch bulb industry, a 32-hectare (79-acre) park which erupts into riotous colour every year from late March to late May. This spectacle, described as 'the greatest flower show on earth', attracts half a million visitors, but the park is big enough to accommodate them all (not so the cafés, however, which get crowded – wise visitors bring a picnic with them).

The wooded park is threaded by a 16-km (10-mile) network of paths, and the potentially garish effect of millions of bulbs is mitigated by skilful planting; variety is provided by the soft green of the woodland putting out new leaves early in the season, followed by the snowy blossoms of Japanese cherry trees and, later in the year, by masses of azalea and rhododendron blooms. The peak of the season occurs at the end of April when there is a huge flower parade on the streets of the nearby town of Lisse.

Keukenhof is located in the heart of the *bloembollenstreek*, the bulb-growing strip, which stretches from Haarlem south to Leiden. This compact area can be explored by bicycle from Leiden, Haarlem or Lisse using maps available from VVV Tourist Information Offices. The cycleways are well marked but can be crowded, especially at weekends. The bulbfields are a spectacular but shortlived sight; commercial growers allow the bulbs to flower just long enough to check that they are true to colour and free from virus and disease. The flowers are then picked, or even mown off, so that the bulb uses its energies in growing new bulbs rather than seed.

The fascinating history of bulb culture in the Netherlands is covered by the **Museum de Zwarte Tulp** (Museum of the Black Tulip) in Lisse (Grachtweg 2A). Here visitors can learn about modern hi-tech production techniques and about the tulip mania that gripped the country after the first bulbs began to be imported from Turkey from 1630; speculation in rare varieties led to massive fortunes being won and lost.

32km (20 miles) southwest of Amsterdam. Getting there: operators compete to offer coach excursions to Keukenhof and the bulbfields, and these can be booked at the VVV Tourist Information Office in Amsterdam. Or buy a day-trip ticket (Rail Idee) from Amsterdam Centraal Station; includes bus transfers from Haarlem and admission charges.
Tourist information: Grachtweg 53A, Lisse. Tel: (0252) 414 262.
Keukenhof tel: (0252) 465 555; www.keukenhof.nl. Open: late Mar–May, daily 8am–7.30pm (last admission 6pm).
Museum de Zwarte Tulp: Grachtweg 2A. Tel: (0252) 417 900; www.museumdezwartetulp.nl. Open: Tue–Sun 1–5pm.

The bulb-growing heart of the Netherlands

Leiden

Leiden is a likeable university town whose numerous museums will fill a full day. The university, the oldest in the Netherlands, was founded in 1574 by William the Silent as a reward for the town's stoicism in the face of a year-long siege by the Spanish. The siege ended only when William broke the dykes around the town, enabling his ships to sail up to the walls on the resulting floodwaters. When the Spanish retreated, the starving citizens climbed the ramparts to find an abandoned pot full of spicy beef and vegetable stew; this dish, *hutspot*, has become the town's speciality.

The university became a major centre of learning and the town still has a studious atmosphere, though its several museums are far from stuffy.

The **Stedelijk Museum de Lakenhal** (Oude Singel 28–32) is a short walk from the station and covers the history of Leiden and especially its cloth-weaving industry, the staple of the local economy until the 18th century. The museum's best-known painting is Lucas van Leyden's *Last Judgement* triptych, and there are numerous rooms furnished in period style.

Nearly opposite (on Tweede Binnenvestgracht 1) is the **Molenmuseum de Valk**, an eight-storey windmill built in 1743, and still working. This museum covers the history of windmills in the Netherlands and provides panoramic city views.

A third museum, the **Rijksmuseum voor Volkenkunde** (National Ethnology Museum), is a short stroll away (Steenstraat 1). Recently, the museum has been restored thoroughly. The rich collection of the objects is displayed in such a way that the visitor will notice both the similarities and the contrast between cultures.

Just south of the museum, on Morspoort, is another windmill, this time a replica of the mill owned by Rembrandt's father, Gerritszoon van Rijn. Rembrandtbrug crosses the River Rijn (Rhine) leading to Weedensteeg where Rembrandt was born in 1606.

Still life with windmill at Leiden

By walking down Rembrandtstraat, left into picturesque Groenhazengracht, then right on Rapenburg, you will come to the university district with its handsome classical buildings, notably the Bibliotheca Thysiana of 1655.

Further down is the entrance to **Hortus Botanicus** (the Botanical Garden, Rapenburg 73), founded in 1575. This delightful spot includes a reconstruction of the original garden, the Clusiustuin, named after the garden's former director, Carolus Clusius, the botanist who first introduced bulbs to the Netherlands.

Another famous Leiden citizen is buried in **Pieterskerk**, on the opposite side of Rapenburg. He is John Robinson, a Puritan refugee from England who settled in Leiden in 1609. He became the leader of the Pilgrim Fathers who set sail from Rotterdam in 1620, bound for the New World. Robinson himself was too ill to join that pioneering voyage and died soon after.

Pieterskerk is surrounded by the narrow lanes of the medieval quarter, and lined with bookshops and peaceful cafés. To the east, Pieterskerkchoorsteeg leads to the main street, Breestraat, and the Renaissance Stadhuis of 1595. To the north, Pieterskerkhof leads to the attractive jumble of buildings that make up Gravensteen, once the court and prison, now the Law Faculty.

Back on Rapenburg you will find the popular **Rijksmuseum van Oudheden** (The National Archaeological Museum). An ancient Egyptian temple has been reconstructed at the entrance, given to the Dutch nation by the Egyptian government. The Temple of Taffeh was originally built in the 1st century AD for sun worship, and converted to Christian use in the 4th century. The museum has a big collection of Egyptian and Roman material and a floor devoted to the archaeology of the Netherlands. *42km (26 miles) southwest of Amsterdam. Getting there: train to Dan Haaz/Rotterdam. Journey time 35 minutes. Tourist information: Stationsweg 2d. Tel: (0900) 222 2333.*

Hortus Botanicus
Rapenburg 73. Tel: (071) 527 7249; www.hortusleiden.nl. Open: Easter–end Oct, daily 10am–6pm; end-Oct–Easter, Sun–Fri 10am–4pm. Closed: Sat, 3 Oct & 25 Dec. Admission charge.
Molenmuseum de Valk
Binnenvestgracht 1. Tel: (071) 516 5353. Open: Tue–Fri 10am–5pm, Sat 11am–5pm, Sun 1–5pm. Closed: Mon, 1 Jan, 3 Oct & 25 Dec. Admission charge.
Pieterskerk
Kloksteeg. Open: daily 1.30–4pm. Free admission.
Rijksmuseum van Oudheden
Rapenburg 28. Tel: (071) 516 3163; www.rmo.nl. Open: Tue–Fri 10am–5pm, Sat, Sun & public holidays noon–5pm. Admission charge.
Rijksmuseum voor Volkenkunde
Steenstraat 1. Tel: (071) 516 8800; www.rmv.nl. Open: Tue–Sun 10am–5pm. Admission charge.
Stedelijk Museum de Lakenhal
Oude Singel 28–32. Tel: (071) 516 5360; www.lakenhal.nl. Open: Tue–Fri 10am–5pm, Sat–Sun noon–5pm.

Marken

Of all the villages on the IJsselmeer north of Amsterdam, Marken is the quietest and most appealing. The local people have reluctantly turned to tourism to save their economy but they remain proud of their distinctive local traditions. Until 1957, Marken was an island, accessible only by boat, and the population of 200 formed an enclosed, strictly Calvinist community largely untouched by the modern world. The way of life of this fishing village began to change with the building of a causeway in 1957 which provided a link to the mainland. Today the population has been increased by incomers to around 2,000.

Long isolation led to a distinctive style of architecture. The pristine wooden houses lining the harbour are a favourite subject for photographers; they are built on stilts as a flood precaution and linked by timber boardwalks. The clapboard façades are painted green and white, while bright red awnings, and scarlet geraniums add to the colourful effect – even the boats moored in the harbour are painted in the same bright colours. Local people still wear traditional costume, especially on religious feast days, and a distinctive feature is the *ryglyf*, a bodice embroidered with intricate floral motifs. Marken has all the appearance of an open-air museum, but it is a living

Marken harbour

village of real atmosphere. Many visitors fall in love with its quiet charms, especially by contrast with the more commercialised village of Volendam, which can be reached from Marken a half-hour boat trip.

18km (11 miles) northeast of Amsterdam. Getting there: bus 111 from Amsterdam Centraal Station, or by boat, the Marken Express, from Volendam or Monnickendam. Tourist information: in Edam, Damplein 1. Tel: (0299) 315 125; www.vvv-edam.nl

Monnickendam

Monnickendam has been described as Amsterdam in miniature. Though little more than a village today, it has some remarkable buildings surviving from a time when Monnickendam was an important trading centre.

The triple-naved **Grote Kerk** dates from the 15th century, and has a fine oak choir screen of 1563. In the narrow lanes of the harbour area, the 15th-century **Speeltoren**, or Clock Tower, now serves as the local museum (**Museum de Speeltoren**, Noordeinde 4); the original clockwork knights in white armour still parade on the hour when the clock carillon plays its delightful tune.

Streets such as Burgwallen, Kerkstraat and Noordeinde are lined with attractive 17th-century houses.

Like other towns on the IJsselmeer, Monnickendam lost its outlet to the sea when the Zuider Zee was dammed, but the enterprising local people quickly turned their hands to fish processing,

The charming town of Monnickendam

specialising in smoked herrings and plump eels. The fragrant smell of woodsmoke lingers in the harbour area where several old-fashioned and informal cafés serve the local speciality – *Monnickendammer twaalf uurtje*, a platter of delicately smoked fish. Another of the town's attractions is the Marken Express, a boat service linking the town with the nearby villages of Marken and Volendam; boats depart at 45-minute intervals during daylight hours from March to October.

16km (10 miles) north of Amsterdam. Getting there: bus 111 from Amsterdam Centraal Station. Journey time 30 minutes. Tourist information: Nieuwpoortslaan 15. Tel: (0299) 651 998. Open: Mon–Fri 9am–5pm, Sat 9am–4pm.
Museum de Speeltoren open: June–mid-Sept, Mon–Sat 10am–4pm, Sun 1–4pm (mid-Apr–May, Sat–Sun only).

Muiderslot

Muiderslot, also known as Muiden Castle, is a beautiful red-brick building that rises from its moat like the archetypal fairy-tale castle. It was originally built in 1285 by a count of Holland, Floris V, who set the economy of medieval Amsterdam on a sound footing by granting its citizens a 'toll privilege' in 1275; this enabled Amsterdammers to transport their goods along the canals of Holland county without paying tolls. Despite – or because of – this, Floris V was kidnapped, imprisoned and finally murdered in his own castle by a group of noblemen angered by his generosity, which had the effect of undermining their income.

The Bishop of Utrecht, who may have been behind the murder conspiracy, annexed the count's territory and demolished the castle in 1296.

The castle was then rebuilt on the same foundations in 1386, and 300 years later it became the residence of Pieter Hooft. Between 1609 and 1647, Hooft, an illustrious poet and historian, used the castle as a place of philosophical and artistic debate. Here he would entertain the leading poets, artists and intellectuals of his day who became known as the Muiden Circle.

After a period of neglect the castle was thoroughly restored in 1948 and it is now furnished in the style of the early 17th century, as it might have been when Monnickendam was a busy merchant port in the time of Pieter Hooft. The charms of the castle are enhanced by delightful gardens.

12km (7 miles) east of Amsterdam. Getting there: bus 136 from Amsterdam Amstel station. Journey time 40 minutes. Herengracht 1. Tel: (0294) 261 325. Open: Apr–Nov, Mon–Sat 10am–5pm, Sun & public holidays 1–5pm; Nov–Apr, Sat–Sun 1–4pm. Closed: Mon–Fri. Guided tours only.

Naarden

Naarden suffered a devastating blow in 1572 when the town was sacked by Spanish troops under Don Frederick of Toledo (son of the Duke of Alva) and almost all the inhabitants were massacred. The brutality of the attack only increased Dutch determination to drive the hated Spaniards from their soil. Naarden was left a ghost town until repopulated in the 17th century when, in order to prevent the possibility of another massacre, the town was equipped with state-of-the-art defences, designed by Adriaan Dortsman. As a result, Naarden has some of the best-preserved Renaissance fortifications in Europe and the town resembles an island surrounded by an impressive double moat and bastions. Their story is told in the **Nederlands Vestingmuseum** (Fortification Museum) located in the Turfpoortbastion (Westwalstraat 6). This is no dry museum of military history but an excellent account of 17th-century warfare; there are subterranean passages to explore, and the admission price includes a boat trip around the moats.

The 1572 massacre is commemorated by a plaque on the **Spaanse Huis** (Spanish House, Turfpoortstraat 27), built in 1615. This now houses the **Comeniusmuseum**, devoted to the life and theories of the philosopher, Johann Komenski (Comenius), a Moravian refugee who settled in the town in 1621 and laid the foundations of modern educational practice; he abhorred learning by rote and was a pioneering advocate of visual aids.

The **Grote Kerk**, in the centre of the town, fortunately survived the Spanish onslaught. It has a wooden choir screen of 1513 and an unusual set of vault paintings illustrating stories from the Old and New Testaments; the 20 wooden panels, painted between 1510 and 1518, are based on the woodcuts of Dürer. The tower is well worth climbing for a bird's-eye view of the fortifications and of the surrounding Gooiland landscape, an extensive area of woodland, heath and lakes.

21km (13 miles) east of Amsterdam. Getting there: bus 136 from Amsterdam Amstel station. Journey time 55 minutes. Tourist information: Adriaan Dortsmanplein 1B. Tel: (035) 694 2836. Nederlands Vestingmuseum: Westwalstraat 6. Tel: (035) 694 5459. Open: 16 Mar–1 Nov, Tue–Fri 10.30am–5pm (and Mon in summer), Sat, Sun & public holidays noon–5pm; Nov–16 Mar, Sun noon–5pm. Grote Kerk open: June–Sept daily 1–4pm. Comeniusmuseum: Kloosterstraat 33. Tel: (035) 694 3045; www.comeniusmuseum.nl. Open: Wed–Sun noon–5pm. Closed: 25 Dec, 31 Dec & 1 Jan.

The turrets and battlements of Muiderslot seem straight from a fairy tale

Rotterdam

Rotterdam was virtually flattened at the beginning of World War II when the Nazis bombed the Netherlands into surrender. A new city has arisen on the old, noted for its imaginative modern architecture, excellent museums and the world's largest container port.

The rather soulless centre is the least attractive part of the city. From the station cross to the windswept pedestrian shopping centre either side of Coolsingel; putting this behind, it is best to head for the waterfront around **Oude Haven** where the most striking of the city's buildings are located.

The pyramidal **Gemeentebibliotheek** (Central Library) clearly owes a debt to the Pompidou Centre in Paris with its external ducting and polished steel. Take a ride on the escalators for views over the old port and of the internal hanging gardens. Alongside are the unusual cube houses designed by Piet Blom; one of them, the **Kijk-Kubus** (Overblaak 70), is open to the public and well worth a visit even if you conclude that the giddying wall angles and the specially adapted furniture make these futuristic houses rather a strain to live in. The complex includes a shop-lined bridge based on the Ponte Vecchio in Florence and the wharf is lined with pleasant cafés.

Further along the boat-filled harbour is the **Maritiem Museum Rotterdam**, devoted to the city's maritime history. The museum ship *De Buffel*, moored alongside, is a 19th-century warship

THE EUROPOORT

Rotterdam's Europoort stretches for 37km (23 miles) along the Nieuwe Maas river and handles some 4 per cent of the world's container traffic. Cargo unloaded here is transported deep into the heart of Europe along three great rivers, the Rhine, the Maas (Meuse) and the Scheldt. Every year around 32,000 ships dock and unload their containers – laid end to end they would stretch for 563,200km (349,956 miles). These and other overwhelming statistics come to life if you take one of the 75-minute Spido harbour tours which depart from Leuvehoofd regularly during the day. *Tel: (010) 275 9988.*

with surprisingly luxurious officers' quarters. If you continue down Leuvehaven you will come to the harbourside offices of Spido Havenrondvaarten, the departure point for boat tours of the Europoort. Further along the waterfront is a distinguished classical building, formerly the Royal Dutch Yacht Club, now a museum of ethnography, the **Wereldmuseum**.

Towering above the adjacent park is the **Euromast**, begun in 1958 for the Floriade flower festival and originally 104m (341ft) high. The Space Tower was added in 1970, bringing the total height to 185m (607ft). External lifts climb to the revolving Space Cabin at the summit where the views take in the whole 37-km (23-mile) waterfront of the Europoort.

Totally different in scale is the Delfshaven district alongside, which escaped bombing and is lined with 18th- and 19th-century warehouses converted to chic apartments.

Maritiem Museum of Rotterdam

Historische Museum Rotterdam (Schielandhuis) *Korte Hoogstraat 31*
De Dubbelde Palmboom
*Voorhaven 12. Tel: (010) 217 6767;
www.hmr.rotterdam.nl. Open: Tue–Fri
10am–5pm, Sat, Sun & public holidays
11am–5pm. Admission charge.*
Euromast
*Parkhaven 20. Tel: (010) 436 4811;
www.euromast.nl. Open: daily, Oct–Mar
10am–11pm, Apr–Sept 9.30am–11pm.
Admission charge.*
Kijk-Kubus
*Overblaak 70. Tel: (010) 414 2285;
www.cubehouse.nl. Open: daily 11am–5pm.
Admission charge.*
Maritiem Museum Rotterdam
*Leuvehaven 1. Tel: (010) 413 2680;
www.maritiemmuseum.nl. Open: Tue–Sat
10am–5pm, Sun & public holidays 11am–5pm;
also Mon 10am–5pm in July & Aug.
Admission charge.*
Museum Boijmans Van Beuningen
*Museumpark 18–20. Tel: (010) 441 9400;
www.boijmans.rotterdam.nl. Open: Tue–Sat
11am–5pm, Sun & public holidays 11am–5pm.
Admission charge.*
Wereldmuseum Rotterdam
*Willemskade 25. Tel: (010) 270 7172;
www.wereldmuseum.rotterdam.nl.
Open: Tue–Sun 10am–5pm. Closed 1 Jan,
30 Apr, 25 Dec. Admission charge.*

The Pilgrim Fathers sailed from here in 1620 in the *Speedwell*; this ship proved unseaworthy and so, after docking at Plymouth, the religious refugees continued to the New World in the *Mayflower*.

De Dubbelde Palmboom (Voorhaven 12) explains the history of the area and its industries, as does **Historische Museum Rotterdam** (Korte Hoogstraat 31).

Returning to the city centre, the **Museum Boijmans Van Beuningen** (Museumpark 18–20) contains one of Europe's most important art collections. Three sections of this vast museum are a must: the rooms dedicated to early Dutch painting contain Pieter Bruegel's *Tower of Babel* and several works by Hieronymus Bosch; rooms 36 and 37 are devoted to

the work of Rembrandt and his pupils; rooms 25 to 30 contain a collection of Surrealistic paintings, including works by Dalí, Magritte and Ernst.
*76km (47 miles) southwest of Amsterdam.
Getting there: train to Rotterdam Coolsingel 67. Journey time 60 minutes.
Tourist information: Coolsingel 67.
Tel: (0900) 403 4065;
www.vvv.rotterdam.nl*

Utrecht

Utrecht is one of the oldest cities in the Netherlands, founded in AD 47 as a Roman garrison town to protect a strategic ford across the River Rhine. Pepin the Short, father of Charlemagne, made Utrecht a bishopric in the 7th century and the city became the main religious centre of the northern Dutch provinces in the Middle Ages, its skyline bristling with the spires of numerous churches and convents. Many were destroyed by a hurricane that hit the town in 1674. Those that remain range in style from Romanesque to High Gothic, several of them now converted to museums.

On arriving in Utrecht visitors first have to negotiate the intrusive 1970s' Hoog Catharijne shopping complex which stands between the station and the old city. Head for **Oude Gracht**, an unusual sunken canal built in two tiers to accommodate the tidal extremes of the Rhine. The lower quay is lined with cavernous cellars, many now turned into cafés and restaurants. Some of Utrecht's oldest buildings line the canal; the Huis Oudaen (No 99) dates from 1320 and Drakenborch (No 114) was built in 1280.

Follow the canal south, heading for the unmissable landmark of the **Domtoren** (Cathedral Tower), a lacy Gothic masterpiece completed in 1382 and soaring to 112m (367ft). Some contemporaries dismissed the tower as a symbol of vanity and pride, predicting that it would surely collapse. In fact, it was the cathedral which came crashing to the ground in the 1674 hurricane, leaving only the choir of 1321, modelled on Cologne Cathedral, and the 15th-century cloister.

The cathedral was conceived as the centrepiece of an ambitious scheme devised by Bishop Bernold in the mid-11th century. He drew up a plan to build five churches, one at each of the four cardinal points of the compass and the cathedral in the centre, together forming the shape of the cross. Only

The Oude Gracht in Utrecht is lined with old buildings and restaurants

two of the five were completed in Bernold's lifetime: to the east of the Domkerk is **Pieterskerk**, built in Romanesque style in 1048, while to the north is **Janskerk**, completed in 1050, and given a new Gothic choir in the 16th century.

From Janskerk, follow the canal delightfully called Drift and then turn left down Kromme Nieuwegracht; this canal follows the original course of the Rhine and is lined with elegant 18th-century houses. It leads to picturesque Pausdam and the late Gothic **Paushuisje** (Pope's House), built in 1517 for Adriaan Floriszoon. He never saw the house, having spent most of his time in Spain as tutor to Charles V and then as the Bishop of Tortosa. In 1622 he became Adrian VI, the first and only Dutch pope – a short-lived reign, as he died the following year.

Nieuwegracht leads south to a former Carmelite convent, now the **Museum Catharijneconvent Utrecht**, whose excellent medieval paintings and sculptures are part of a collection illustrating the history of religion in the Netherlands. Further south, the **Centraal Museum**, housed in another medieval convent, has an eclectic range of exhibits, ranging from period rooms, costumes and doll's houses, to the Renaissance paintings of the Utrecht artist Jan van Scorel, and the colourful modern furniture of the de Stijl movement architect Gerrit Rietveld. Train enthusiasts should not miss the **Nederlands Spoorwegmuseum**

(Railway Museum), housed nearby in the disused 19th-century station.

The best route back to the city centre is through the park alongside Stads-buitengracht, formerly the moat of the medieval city walls, then up Springweg to Buurkerkhof. This 13th-century church now houses the **Nationaal Museum Van Speelklok tot Pierement** (meaning From Musical Clocks to Street Organs), an enchanting museum of mechanical musical instruments.
35km (22 miles) south of Amsterdam. Getting there: train to Utrecht CS. Journey time 30 minutes. Tourist information: Vinkenburgstraat 19. Tel: (0900) 128 8732; www.utrechtstad.com

Centraal Museum
Nicolaaskerkhof 10. Tel: (030) 236 2362; www.centraalmuseum.nl. Open: Tue–Sun noon–5pm, Fri noon–9pm. Closed 1 Jan, 30 Apr, 25 Dec. Admission charge.
Domtoren
Domplein. Tel: (030) 286 4540. Open: Mon–Sat 10am–4pm, Sun noon–4pm. Admission charge.
Nationaal Museum Van Speelklok tot Pierement
Steenweg 6. Tel: (030) 231 2789; www.museumspeelklok.nl. Open: Tue–Sun and holidays 10am–5pm. Closed 1 Jan, 30 Apr, 25 Dec. Admission charge.
Nederlands Spoorwegmuseum
Maliebaanstation. Tel: (030) 230 6206; www.spoorwegmuseum.nl. Open: Tue–Sun 10am–5pm, also Mon during school holidays. Closed 1 Jan and 30 Apr. Admission charge.
Museum Catharijneconvent Utrecht
Lange Nieuwstraat 38. Tel: (030) 231 3835; www.catharijneconvent.nl. Open: Tue–Fri 10am–5pm, Sat, Sun & public holidays 11am–5pm. Admission charge.

Volendam

The former fishing village of Volendam is now a highly commercialised tourist attraction, to be avoided by those who do not like crowds and shops full of kitsch souvenirs (go to quieter Marken or Monnickendam instead). On the other hand, it is fun for children and the local people are friendly, wholehearted participants in this recreation of 'old world' Holland. Like actors in a living theme park, they pose for photographers in village costume – baggy black trousers for the men and winged lace caps and striped aprons for the women. Visitors are also welcome to dress up in costume and have their pictures taken. The harbour is lined with picturesque wooden houses, and the **Volendams Museum** (Kloostervuurt 5) tells the story of the local fishing industry.

18km (11 miles) northeast of Amsterdam. Getting there: bus 110, 112 & 116 from Amsterdam Centraal Station. Journey time 30 minutes. Or buy a day-trip excursion ticket which includes the bus journey to Edam, plus boat transfers to Marken and Volendam.
Tourist information: Zeestraat 41. Tel: (0299) 369 258; www.vvv-volendam.nl; Volendams Museum open: daily, Mar–Nov 10am–5pm.
Admission charge.

Zaanse Schans

The former villages of Zaandam, Koog aan de Zaan and Zaandijk, north of Amsterdam, all take their names from the River Zaan on whose banks they sit. An industrial revolution of a kind occurred here in the 16th century with the invention of a wind-powered sawmill: the area became the biggest supplier of timber for shipbuilding and house construction in the Netherlands. When Monet came here to paint the scene in the 1870s there were over 1,000 windmills producing everything from corn and mustard to paint pigments and vegetable oil. Development has continued and the former villages have merged to form the Zaanstad conurbation. In the 1950s, many of the surviving windmills were moved to the Zaanse Schans, located on the river bank opposite Zaandijk. An unusual feature of the open-air museum is that people actually live in its houses and windmills, and several of the mills continue to produce mustard and flour. They are maintained in pristine working order by enthusiasts who lovingly demonstrate the complex workings of these elegant machines. The museum also has several streets of 17th-century timber-gabled houses where visitors can watch craft demonstrations, and take a boat trip along the River Zaan.

14km (9 miles) north of Amsterdam. Getting there: train from Amsterdam Centraal Station to Koog-Zaandijk. Journey time 15 minutes.
Visitor's Centre Vrede: Schansend 1, Zaandam. Tel: (075) 616 8218; www.zaanseschans.nl.
Open: daily 9am–5pm.

Zandvoort

On hot summer days when Amsterdammers feel like a cooling dip in the sea they head for Zandvoort, a popular coastal resort but big enough to accommodate the crowds with ease. The busiest beaches are those closest to Zandvoort town, whose northern quarter has been conserved and retains the atmosphere of a fishing village. The modern part of the town has numerous fish restaurants, and a casino (Badhuisplaats) worth a visit just for the views. Sandy and gently shelving beaches stretch for kilometres either side of the town and you will find privacy if you walk far enough. Nature lovers should head south to the **Waterleidingduinen**, an undulating dune reserve where horned poppy and sea holly grow in the sheltered lee of the shifting sandbanks.

25km (16 miles) west of Amsterdam. Getting there: train from Amsterdam Centraal Station to Zandvoort aan Zee. Journey time 24 minutes. Tourist information: Schoolplein 1. Tel: (023) 571 7947; www.vvvzk.nl

Zandvoort: a nearby getaway for Amsterdammers

Amsterdam environs

Getting away from it all

'*I like to wander through the old narrow and rather sombre streets with their shops occupied by chemists, lithographers and ship's chandlers and browse among the navigation charts and other ship's supplies. I cannot tell you how beautiful the area is at twilight.*'

VINCENT VAN GOGH

Amsterdamse Bos (Amsterdam Woods)

Amsterdam Woods, on the southern fringes of the city, is the product of the Great Depression of the 1930s. To resolve the problem of mass unemployment, the city decided to convert 895 hectares (2,212 acres) of polder into a recreation park modelled on the Bois de Boulogne in Paris. No machinery was used in making the park, so as to create the maximum number of jobs.

The park is man-made in a very real sense: teams of men and horses laid 310km (193 miles) of drainage pipe to lower the water table by 1.5m (5ft) so that the thousands of trees they planted would develop strong roots. They dug the Roeibaan, a 2km (1-mile) rowing lake, created an artificial hill to act as a viewpoint and laid over 200km (124 miles) of footpaths and cycle tracks.

The result today is a mature park, beautifully maintained, where visitors can escape the crowds and wander along tree-shaded paths, picnic in sunny glades or by the lakeside, hire a bicycle, go canoeing or swim in the lake. Those who simply want to walk can follow the Roeibaan to its furthest point and visit the Bosmuseum (Woodland Museum) which explains how the park was built and illustrates all its flora and fauna, from squirrels and songbirds to fungi and 700 different beetle species.

Entrance: Bosmuseum, Koenenkade 56.
Tel: (020) 676 2152.
Park open: 24 hours.
Museum open: daily 10am–5pm.
Free admission. Bus: 170, 171 & 172. Or take tram 6 or 16, or bus 15, to Haarlemmermeer station and ride to the park on an old-fashioned tram. (Services every Sun, Apr–Oct, also Tue–Sat in July–Aug; see Electrische Museumtramlijn, p49, for details.)

Hortus Botanicus Plantage (Botanical Garden)

Laid out in 1682 as a medicinal garden, it soon evolved into a showcase for the many new plants that Dutch explorers brought back from the Far East. In 1706, it became the first place outside Arabia to cultivate the coffee plant.

The main features of this garden are a Palm House of iron and glass with aerial walkways, which houses the world's oldest pot plant, a 400-year-old palm, an Orangery where you can enjoy coffee and cakes, a herb garden in the 17th-century style, a huge hothouse which incorporates three different tropical climates, a special area for carnivorous plants, a rock garden, a Japanese garden and an educational house.

Plantage Middenlaan 2a.
Tel: (020) 625 9021; www.dehortus.nl.
Mon–Fri opens 9am, Sat–Sun and hols opens 10am; closes 9pm in July–Aug, and
5pm other months. Closed: 1 Jan & 25 Dec. Admission charge.
Tram: 7, 9 & 14. Nearby: Zoo (Artis).

Hortus Botanicus Van de Vrije Universiteit (Botanical Garden of the Free University)

This garden was planted in 1967. It has an interesting section devoted to the native flora of the Netherlands, large areas of woodland and glasshouses devoted to cold, temperate or tropical-climate plants.

Van der Boechorststraat 8. Tel: (020) 444 9390; www.vv.nl/hortus. Open: Mon–Fri 8am–4.30pm; also July–Aug Sat 9am–5pm.
Free admission. Bus: 23, 65, 170, 171, 172 & 199. Nearby: Amsterdamse Bos.

Getting away from it all

The unspoilt beauty of Amsterdamse Bos

Cost-effective, 'green' family transport

Cycle routes

Every year thousands of visitors to Amsterdam are seduced into believing that 'cycling is the ideal means of transport in Amsterdam'. They hire a bike and then wish they had not. Cycling in Amsterdam is a hair-raising experience; bike-riding natives are a law unto themselves: everybody seems to ignore the traffic rules, including pedestrians, and when you reach for your brakes you often find they are not there – many Dutch bikes are the old-fashioned kind which you have to back-pedal to stop. Bicycles are also a favourite target of thieves who find ways of removing even the most securely locked bikes. With practice all these problems can be overcome, but if you do choose to cycle in Amsterdam, dismount at busy intersections and cross on foot, and secure your bike to an immovable object if you leave it in the street.

By contrast, cycling in the Dutch countryside is a joy, especially in summer when there is no wind to fight against. The rider has the choice of over 10,000km (6,214 miles) of specially designated cycle paths (*fietspaden*), which are clearly marked on ANWB 1:100,000 scale maps and well signposted on the ground. Road and cycleway intersections are usually numbered so you can always find out where you are on the map. VVV Tourist Information Centres also supply informative maps of local cycle routes. You can hire bicycles at almost any railway station – a system designed to discourage people from taking their own bikes on the trains. Simply present your ticket if you have one and some means of identification, such as a passport, at the ticket office; you will be charged a small refundable deposit and a negligible hire fee; children's bikes and bikes with child seats can also be hired.

Several nature reserves within easy reach of Amsterdam offer traffic-free cycling conditions, as well as scenic landscapes, picnic spots and wildlife. From the station at Castricum (26km/16 miles) northwest of Amsterdam; journey time 30 minutes) you are within easy reach of the **North Holland Dunes**, an extensive area of sand and shingle bank backed by thick woodland. Johanna's Hof, at the highest point in the woods, is a very popular destination because of its pancakes and small zoo.

To the east of Amsterdam you can take a train to **Hilversum** (20km/12 miles); journey time 20 minutes) and explore the extensive heath and woodland of the Bussummerheide and Boswachterij De Lage Vuursche, heading for the pancake houses in the village of Lage Vuursche when you are hungry.

The rolling hills and moors of the **Nationaal Park Hoge Veluwe**, north of Arnhem (*see p102*), are ideal for cycling, and free bikes, painted white, are available for anyone to use within the confines of the vast park. Hoge Veluwe has the added attraction of its open-air **Sculpture Garden** and the **Kröller-Müller Museum**, featuring over 200 Van Gogh paintings.

Once confident enough to cope with the roads, you could visit the IJsselmeer villages of Marken and Monnickendam (*see pp120–21*) by bike instead of by bus or coach (maps available from the Amsterdam VVV). If you hire a bike at Amsterdam Centraal Station, you can cross the IJ harbour by free passenger ferry. The ferry departs regularly from the harbour side of the station (signposted Pont naar Tolhuis). You

will initially encounter traffic on the northern bank but, as you cycle east along Durgerdammerdijk, the suburbs give way to open countryside dotted with red-roofed farmhouses and you may spot herons wading in the watercourses.

The route passes through Durgerdam, an attractive former fishing village, then along the shores of the IJsselmeer to Uitdam; 3km (2 miles) further on is the causeway to the island village of **Marken** with its painted wooden houses, and beyond lies **Monnickendam**, 'Amsterdam in miniature'.

The return journey is through **Broek in Waterland**, a town of spotless beauty and a major centre of cheese production, where the informal restaurant, De Witte Swaen, is used by hungry cyclists. From here the road through Zunderdorp will bring you back to the IJ ferry. Allow at least four hours for the 34km (21-mile) round trip.

The humble bicycle has found its niche in the flat, narrow streets, alleys and bridges of Amsterdam

Maritime exhibits in the Rykers Museum at Den Helder

Den Helder and the Waddenzee

From Amsterdam Centraal Station it is only an hour by train to Den Helder, a port town on the edge of a truly wild corner of the Netherlands renowned for its bird and marine life. Ferries from Den Helder cross to the island of Texel, the first and largest of the five Frisian (or Wadden) Islands which extend in a broad curve eastwards to the German coast. These islands, and the submerged sandbars in between, act as a natural breakwater, separating the shallow waters of the Waddenzee to the east from the rough and often stormy North Sea to the west.

The Waddenzee covers an area of almost 2,600sq km (1,004sq miles), but is nowhere more than 3m (10ft) deep, even at high tide. As the tide goes out the sea rolls away to expose an extensive area of mudflats rich in marine molluscs, worms and the spawn of numerous North Sea fish. This in turn attracts huge feeding flocks of gulls, waders and wildfowl.

Den Helder itself was a fishing village until Napoleon fortified it as a naval base in 1808, and it remains the headquarters of the Dutch naval fleet. Ferries to Texel depart from the harbour at hourly intervals all through the year and the crossing takes 20 minutes.

From the island port of 't Horntje, buses go to **Den Burg**, the main village, where visitors can hire bicycles, see the local museum and then call at the VVV Tourist Information Centre (*Emmalaan 66, tel: (0222) 314 741*) for a guide to cycle routes and to the island's numerous bird sanctuaries. **De Koog**, on the western side of Texel, is the island's main resort and has a small natural history centre, the Ecomare, with a bird and seal sanctuary and aquarium, but the best spots for birdwatching lie to the south and east, below Den Hoorn.

Depending on the season, visitors should look out for waders such as curlews, oystercatchers, plovers, redshanks, greenshanks and stints, as well as pintail ducks, shelducks, teal, terns and geese. Sadly, the grey seals that were once so common are now a rare sight. A viral disease has decimated the population and the remaining colonies are limited to the less-populated of the Frisian Islands.

Island hopping and mudwalking

The best way to explore the **Frisian Islands** is by hiring an antique sailing boat for the week or a weekend, complete with crew and sleeping accommodation (*details from Rederij Vooruit, Geeuwkade 9, 8651 AA IJlst; tel:*

(0515) 531 485; www.rederij-vooruit.nl). Otherwise the islands can be reached only by separate ferries from the mainland.

You can also walk to some of the islands on *wadlopen* (mudwalking) excursions during summer, but for that you must be physically fit, and quite prepared to get very muddy: wading up to your thighs in mud is as demanding as mountain climbing. It is dangerous to cross the mudflats on your own, so join a party led by an officially licensed guide if you want a close encounter with the rich and varied ecology of the Waddenzee (*details from Dijkstra's Wadlooptochten, Hoofdstraat 118, 9968 AM Pieterburen; tel: (0595) 528 345).*

As a rule, the five Frisian Islands become smaller, wilder and more remote from civilisation the further north you travel, although they can be busy on summer weekends when sunbathers and windsurfers pour out of the cities to enjoy them.

Texel is the only island where visitors will encounter cars in any number. **Vlieland** (reached by ferry from Harlingen) is popular with birdwatchers and naturists – it has the biggest nudist beach in Europe.

Terschelling, the middle island (also reached from Harlingen), once guarded the main shipping lanes into the Zuider Zee; numerous ships were wrecked on its shifting sandbanks, including the *Lutine*, whose bell, the only part recovered, is still rung at Lloyd's, the London insurance market, whenever a ship is declared lost at sea.

Dunes at Terschelling beach

Shopping

Amsterdam, a city built on commerce, seems at first glance to have surprisingly few shops, until you realise that they are, very sensibly, tucked away on pedestrianised side streets or along the short radial canals that link the three main canals of the Grachtengordel. Here you will find all sorts of surprises: Amsterdam's shopkeepers are masters of the art of window display and there are many small speciality shops that sell a single product in all its varieties.

It is easy to spend a whole day shopping or browsing and not be bored. Thursday is best, as the shops stay open until 9pm. Saturday is the busiest day, but shops close around 5pm and many do not reopen until 1pm (department stores 11am) on Monday. Increasingly, shops are opening on Sunday, usually from noon to 5pm, but fewer shops are open on Monday morning. Otherwise, normal shopping hours are between 9am and 6pm, and most major credit cards are universally accepted.

SHOPPING IN THE CENTRE

Damrak, the main street of Amsterdam, is dominated by fast-food outlets and souvenir shops, and is a major eyesore and blight on a charming city. Escape into one of the cafés in **De Bijenkorf** (The Beehive). The Harrods of Amsterdam, it sells everything from Delftware to handmade chocolates, though you may find certain clothes cheaper at the **C & A** and **Peek &**

Cloppenburg stores on Damrak and Dam Square, respectively.

Parallel to Damrak is Nieuwendijk, a crowded pedestrian precinct lined with cheap clothes shops and brightly lit stalls selling doughnuts and nougat that would not look out of place in a fairground.

Opposite, the former main Post Office has been turned into the up-market 200-shop **Magna Plaza** galleria providing a new shopping focus to the city. Just to the right of Magna Plaza, on the tiny Molsteeg (No 4), is **Christopher Clarke**, where beautiful earrings are designed and made on the premises.

Kalverstraat, the main shopping street in the city, runs from Dam Square to Muntplein. Competition between traders is fierce and there are many bargains to be had if you shop around in the high-street fashion stores. Some well-known multinational chains also have branches here: **Hennes & Mauritz** at No 125, **Body Shop** at

Nos 157–9 and **Waterstone's Booksellers** at No 152. At the junction of Kalverstraat and Spui you can see the splendid Empire-style building recently given a modern, hi-tech interior for the popular fashion chain, **Esprit**.

Just a few steps away at Spui 12 is the new location of **The American Book Center**, with a huge stock of international magazines and English-language books.

On Muntplein, alongside the Munttoren, is **De Porceleyne Fles**, the official outlet for genuine handpainted Delftware, marked on the base with the letter D, a considerably superior product to the cheap mass-produced blue and white pottery sold as Delft in many souvenir shops.

A few steps away, on Singel, is the **Bloemenmarkt** (Flower Market), where florists sell bulbs, seeds, floral bouquets and even clipped box topiary from floating stalls. The florists can advise on customs regulations concerning the import of plant materials and will arrange shipping. In December, christmas trees are also on sale.

Turning left at the end of Singel brings you to Koningsplein and Leidsestraat, another busy shopping thoroughfare. The highlight here is **Metz & Co**, which sells the products of top international designers – furniture, fabrics, kitchenware, glass and smaller gift items such as ornaments and toiletries.

The striking postmodern café on the top floor is an excellent place to rest your weary feet and enjoy the fine views.

The 'Beehive' is a honeypot for shoppers

Markets

Albert Cuypstraat is the venue for Amsterdam's main market (Mon–Sat 9.30am–5pm), a crowded, colourful, and vibrant affair attended by up to 50,000 people on a typical Saturday. The stalls and milling crowds stretch for just over a kilometre, making this Europe's biggest general market. It occupies the heart of the district known as the 'Pijp' – the Pipe – because the long, narrow and slightly curving streets resemble the stem of an old-fashioned clay pipe.

The market has a festive social air because people come here to be seen and to meet friends as much as to shop. The eye is one moment diverted by the stalls piled high with exotic fish and vegetables, colourful cheeses and bolts of fabric, the next by the passing parade of people of all races that make up this multi-ethnic city.

Many visitors look for traditional clogs to take home

Local cheese

Albert Cuypstraat sells useful things – clothes, food, even livestock and pets – whereas Amsterdam's other big market, on Waterlooplein (Mon–Sat 9am–5pm), is a flea market in the very real sense, but it still makes for fascinating browsing and just occasionally you might pick up an Art Deco vase, a mirror or some knick-knack that you cannot resist. Bargaining over the price is all part of the fun. Amsterdam has several other markets along the same lines, selling books, old records and near antiques – on Noordermarkt every Monday

Jenever bottles

7.30am–1pm and Saturday 9am–4pm. Visit the indoor arcade called Antiekcentrum de Looier, entered from Elandsgracht 109 (Sat–Thur 11am–5pm). Less well known by visitors, but interesting, are the Sunday art markets held on the Spui and Thorbeckeplein (both Apr–Nov only, 10am–6pm).

Stamp and coin collectors should visit the specialist market on Nieuwezijds Voorburgwal (Wed & Sat 1–4pm), while every Friday on the Spui square (in front of the American Book Center) is an open-air market for second-hand books, mostly in Dutch (open daily 10am–5pm). Finally, all self-respecting greens and ecologists do their weekly shopping at the Boerenmarkt (Farmers' Market) on Noordermarkt (Sat 9am–4pm, 3pm in winter) where all the produce on sale is organic.

Ironically there is another, far from ecological, market alongside; the weekly pet market.

Waterlooplein market is a fascinating place to browse for exotica

Cheese shop selling local cheeses

SPECIALITY SHOPS

Characterful small shops are to be found all over Amsterdam, especially along the quiet, village-like streets of the Canal Circle, known as the 'Negen Straatjes', or Nine Streets, for the streets which run parallel between the three main canals. Here you are likely to find just the gift (for yourself, or for friends) that proved so elusive in the busier shopping thoroughfares. This directory is by no means exhaustive, but it does cover some of the most distinctive shops in the city.

Antiques

The Spiegelkwartier is renowned for its concentration of antique shops where you can pick up relatively inexpensive Dutch tiles or spend a fortune on an Old Master. In **Nieuwe Spiegelstraat**, Kunsthandel Aalderink (No 15)

specialises in oriental and ethnographic art; **Inez Stodel** (No 65) specialises in period jewellery and decorative objects; **Frides Lameris** (No 55) in fine glass dating to the 17th century; **Aronson Antiquairs** (No 39) specialises in 17th- and 18th-century continental furniture and rare Delftware. **Van Nie Antiquairs**, around the corner at Keizersgracht 600, is known for Dutch furniture and Delftware from the 17th and 18th centuries.

The prices are slightly lower in Kerkstraat where **De Bres** (No 179) features a selection of paintings by Dutch, French and Russian artists – Impressionistic, figurative and realistic. **Lambiek** (No 132) sells thousands of antique comics and the original drawings of comic artists and cartoonists.

Outside the Spiegelkwartier, **'t Winkeltje** (Prinsengracht 228) is a wonderful jumble of inexpensive antique toys, bottles, lamps, crystal and candlesticks.

Books

The Book Exchange (Kloveniersburgwal 42) sells second-hand English-language titles and will accept your unwanted books in part exchange. **Architectura et Natura** (Leliegracht 22) has a comprehensive stock of books in every language on architecture, wildlife and gardening. **Athenaeum** (Spui 14–16) stocks the city's widest range of non-fiction titles and international periodicals. **Jacob van Wijngaarden** (Overtoom 97) is the best for maps and guidebooks to anywhere in the world.

Cakes and confectionery

Arnold Cornelis (Van Baerlestraat 93) has ravishing window displays and specialises in up-market patisserie and handmade chocolates.

Camera supplies

Schweizer Foto (Haarlemmerdijk 114).

Candles

Kramer Pontifex (Reestraat 20) sells nothing but candles from all over the world in an extraordinary range of colours and shapes – works of art in wax that you will not want to set alight.

Cheese

Wegewijs Kaas (Rozengracht 32) proves that there is far more to Dutch cheese than Edam and Gouda; **Kef** (Marnixstraat 192) has a superb range of French farmhouse cheeses, and is ideal for picnic supplies since it also sells wine, baguettes, sausages and pâtés.

Chocolates

Puccini (Staalstraat 17) makes beautiful chocolates using the finest cocoa. While at **Pompadour** (Huidenstraat 12) you can indulge in rich pastries in the tearoom before buying handmade chocolates, including the truffle specialities.

Cigars and tobacco

PGC Hajenius (Rokin 92–6) is renowned for its old-world atmosphere, its own brand of cigars and its huge collection of pipes.

Clogs

De Klompenboer (St Antoniesbreestraat 51) makes serious clogs (Klompen) that are meant to be worn, and decorative painted versions for hanging on the wall.

Clothes

Couturiers and boutiques in PC Hooftstraat cater for the moneyed end of the market: typical designer icons from Chanel and Gucci to Vuitton and Dolce and Gabbana are on display. For more affordable high-street fashions, popular spots are **America Today**, **Magna Plaza shopping mall** (behind Dam Square) and Sarphatistraat 48 or **Esprit** (Spui 1c). Cheaper still are shops specialising in vintage or antique garments, such as **Lady Day** (Hartenstraat 9) and **Laura Dols** (Wolvenstraat 7) whose stock includes real collector's items.

A window for the discerning cigar smoker

Glassware, a decorative memento of Amsterdam

Condoms

The **Condomerie het Gulden Vlies** (Warmoesstraat 141) presents its mind-boggling collection with style. Discreet staff offer advice and information.

Ethnic art

Baobab (Elandsgracht 128) sells jewellery, furniture and carpets from the Far East.

Fabrics and trimmings

Capsicum (Oude Hoogstraat 1) specialises in Thai silks and Indian cottons; **Knopen Winkel** (Herengracht 383) in buttons from all over the world; and the **Albert Cuyp market** (*see p138*) is also an excellent place to buy clothes and fabrics.

Glass and ceramics

The Galleria d'Arte 'Rinascimento' (Prinsengracht 170) specialises in antique and reproduction Delftware and Makkum pottery and the stock ranges from thimbles to tile paintings, tulip vases and apothecaries' jars. **Glasgalerie Kuhler** (Prinsengracht 134) stocks art glass by leading makers at surprisingly reasonable prices.

Herbal remedies

Jacob Hooy (Kloveniersburgwal 12) sells homeopathic remedies from an original apothecary's shop established in 1743. The stock includes a vast range of culinary herbs and spices, plant-based cosmetics and health foods.

Lace

The genuine article, handmade rather than machine-produced Dutch lace, can be bought at **Het Kantenhuis** (Kalverstraat 124).

Leather clothing

Designer **Marianne Vanderwilt**
(Geldersekade 43) creates fashionable
leather jackets, trousers, dresses and
skirts for a hip, international clientele.

Models

The Scale Train House (Bilderdijkstraat
94) sells far more than its name
suggests: do-it-yourself construction
kits of everything from windmills and
three-masted sailing ships to moon-
landing craft, as well as a huge stock of
railway engines, track and scenery.

Plants

Amsterdam's famous **Bloemenmarkt**
(Flower Market) stretches along the
Singel Canal from Muntplein to
Koningsplein. The 15 florists based here
sell a vast range of cut flowers and
bulbs. They also sell pot plants;
however, check with the stallholders
whether the plants you buy are
exportable. (*Open: Mon–Sat 9.30am–
6pm, up to 5pm on Sat.*) Also worth
visiting for a range of unusual cut
flowers and bouquets are **Pompon
Bloemenwinkel** (Prinsengracht 8)
and **Gerda's Bloemen & Planten**
(Runstraat 16).

Postcards and posters

All of Amsterdam's three main
museums sell first-class reproductions
of the art in their collections. **Art
Unlimited** (Keizersgracht 510) has
an enormous stock from around
the world.

Tea and coffee

Geels en Co (Warmoesstraat 67)
products scent the whole street; the
shop is a museum of the history of tea
and coffee making and historic
packaging. Another specialist shop,
Simon Levelt (Prinsengracht 180), has
a vast stock of teas and coffees and old
tiled interior.

Teeth

De Witte Tandenwinkel or The White
Teeth Shop (Runstraat 5) is an eccentric
but successful outlet for everything to
do with dental hygiene; champagne-
flavoured toothpaste and novelty
tooth-brushes are among the
best-selling lines.

Toys

Beautifully made toys in wood are a
Dutch speciality and many are
bought by collectors who have no
intention of allowing them to become
play-worn. They can be found at
Tesselschade Arbeid Adelt
(Leidseplein 33).

At **Kramer** (Reestraat 20) the owner
restores old (and new) dolls and
teddy bears.

Videos

Cine-Qua-Non (Staalstraat 14) is a
film-lovers' haven, stocking videotapes
of cult and art movies that are not
widely available on the commercial
market, as well as all kinds of posters,
magazines, books and memorabilia to
do with the cinema.

Diamonds

Amsterdam has been an important centre for diamond processing since the 17th century. The industry was founded by Jewish refugees who were prohibited from joining the well-established city guilds, which effectively barred them from many areas of employment. They therefore pursued trades which were not regulated – retail trading, banking, printing and diamond working. From these roots the industry blossomed, partly due to the skill of Amsterdam's diamond cutters and polishers, and partly because the Dutch colonies in South Africa proved to be such a rich source of raw diamonds. This led to a boom during the 1870s when diamond processing became the city's fastest-growing sector.

Today Amsterdam's diamond companies concentrate on the jewellery trade since artificial diamonds, invented in the 1950s, are now used for most industrial applications. Several companies offer workshop tours where visitors may learn how rough diamonds are turned

The Gassan Diamonds building

Diamonds are forever: Amsterdam has been known for perfect diamond processing skills since the 17th century

into sparkling gems. You will discover the factors that influence the price. These are the four Cs of the diamond trade: the colour (diamonds can be green, blue, rose, yellow or brown as well as pure white), the cut (the number of facets), the clarity (dictated by the number and size of inclusions) and the carat (the weight; 1 carat = 0.2gm/0.007oz). Visitors are also sure to be told about the world's biggest diamond, the Cullinan (found in South Africa, 1905), which weighed 3,106 carats in its rough state: it was cut into 105 separate gems of which the largest, Cullinan I (530 carats), the world's largest cut diamond, occupies pride of place as the central jewel in the British crown.

The following companies give free guided tours on request:

Amsterdam Diamond Centre
Rokin 1–5. Tel: (020) 624 5787;
www.amsterdamdiamondcentre.nl.
Open: Mon–Wed, Fri–Sat 10am–6pm,
Thur 10am–8.30pm, Sun 11am–6pm.

Coster Diamonds
Paulus Potterstraat 2–8. Tel: (020) 305
5555; www.costerdiamonds.com.
Open: daily 9am–5pm.

Gassan Diamonds
Nieuwe Uilenburgerstraat 173–5.
Tel: (020) 622 5333;
www.gassandiamonds.com.
Open: daily 9am–5pm.

Entertainment

Amsterdam's lively entertainment scene caters to every taste. At least 14,000 theatrical performances or concerts are said to take place in the city every year, which works out to an average of 40 a day. The VVV Amsterdam Tourist Office publishes a useful monthly listings magazine, Day by Day, *which specifically concentrates on events that can be enjoyed by English-speaking visitors.*

Cinema

Almost all films are shown in their original language versions (predominantly English), all with Dutch subtitles; the few exceptions that are only shown in Dutch will feature the words *Nederlands Gesproken* on the poster. Several cinemas mount special afternoon matinees featuring cartoons, science fiction or children's films. Some cinemas still have an interval in the middle of the film. Cinema listings are found in numerous bars and cafés and in the free newspaper for expats, *The Amsterdam Weekly*.

Cinecenter

This small multiplex cinema usually shows a couple of English-language films. Unfortunately they insist on having an intermission for smokers.
Lijnbaansgracht 236. Tel: (020) 6236615.

The Movies

A cosy neighbourhood cinema specialising in international art movies and classics, with an authentic 1930s café.

Haarlemmerdijk 161.
Tel: (020) 638 6016. Tram: 3.

Nederlands Filmmuseum

The films shown here are drawn from the museum's archives, everything from silent movies (shown with live piano accompaniment) to the art films of Truffaut and Tarkovsky – the whole gamut of European cinema, in fact, and with three different films a day there is plenty of choice. In summer, the terrace of this 19th-century former tea room is used for outdoor screenings.

Note: they will be moving to a new location opposite the water behind Centraal Station around the end of 2009.

Vondelpark 3. Tel: (020) 589 1400;
www.filmmuseum.nl. Box office
open: Mon–Fri 9am–10pm, Sat–Sun 2–10pm. Tram: 1, 2, 3, 5 & 12.

Pathé de Munt

The biggest cinema in Amsterdam with eleven screens; expect to queue at weekends for popular blockbuster movies.

The Art Deco façade of the Tuschinski cinema

Leidseplein. Tel: (0900) 1458.
Tram: 1, 2, 5, 7 & 10.

Pathé Tuschinski

Worth visiting just for its beautiful
and authentic 1920s interior in the
main hall. Amsterdam's showcase
cinema, used for celebrity premieres,
also has a few smaller halls. Expect
queues at weekends if you have not
booked in advance.
Reguliersbreestraat 26.
Tel: (020) 626 2633.
Box office open: daily noon–10pm.
Tram: 4, 9 & 14.

Rialto

This arthouse cinema has some
English-language films and attracts
an international crowd. Café on
the premises.
Ceintuurbaan 338.
Tel: (020) 676 8700.

Classical music, ballet and opera

Beurs Van Berlage

Amsterdam's former stock and
commodities exchange is now a cultural
centre, home to the Netherlands
Philharmonic and Chamber Orchestras
who perform in two superbly converted
halls named after the commercial
sponsors, the AGA Zaal and the Wang
Zaal. Concerts cover the whole musical
repertoire and occasionally feature top
international soloists.
Damrak 277. Tel: (020) 521 7575; for
tickets: 0900 0191; www.berlage.com.
Box office open: Tue–Fri 2–5pm and two
hours before a performance.
Tram: 4, 9, 16, 24 & 25.

Bimhuis

This Amsterdam legend has hosted
many of the top names in jazz over the
years. In its modern new setting, the

soul remains along with the open seating. There is a restaurant for guests with tickets to the concert. Free jam sessions and 'jazz clinics' are often held. *Piet Heinkade 3. Tel: (020) 788 2150. Tram: 25 & 26 or 5-min walk from Centraal Station.*

Churches

The Engelsekkerk (Begijnhof 48; *tel: (020) 624 9665; www.ercadam.nl*) hosts free lunchtime concerts in July and August, and evening concerts throughout the year. Look out for occasional organ recitals and choral concerts in Oude Kerk (Oudekerksplein 23; *tel: (020) 625 8284; www.oudekerk.nl*) and Nieuwe Kerk (Dam Square*; tel: (020) 638 6909; www.nieuwekerk.nl*). The Waalse Kerk (Oudezijds Achterburgwal 157; *tel: (020) 623 2074*) is used for early music recitals, and the Ronde Lutherse

Kerk (Kattengat 1) hosts occasional Sunday-morning recitals.

Concertgebouw

In contrast to the Muziektheater, the Concertgebouw is renowned for its acoustics, which are exploited to the full by the Royal Concertgebouw Orchestra, internationally famous for performances of the big rich works of Mahler, Strauss, Ravel and Debussy. In 2004 the orchestra appointed a new conductor, the Latvian-born Mariss Jansons. A second smaller hall is used for chamber works. There are often jazz concerts held here too! Concerts are popular, so advance booking is advisable. *Concertgebouwplein 2–6. Tel: (02) 671 8345; www.concertgebouw.nl. Box office open: daily 10am–7pm, by phone till 5pm. Tram: 3, 5 & 16.*

Concertgebouw is filled with the rich sound of masters

Muziekgebouw aan't IJ

Opened by the Queen in June 2005, this audaciously modern music centre literally lights up the Docklands area at night. As with most challenging modern buildings, it has both its friends and its critics, but at a cost of €52 million it is hoped that it will succeed in pleasing both the people of Amsterdam and the city's many visitors.

This is no conventional music centre, with an auditorium, a bar and a bookshop. For a start, it has opened its arms and welcomed the city's main jazz club, Bimhuis, which has moved here from its former warehouse home. The IJsbreker concert hall-cum-café, home to many progressive modern works, has also relocated to the Muziekgebouw. The children's KlankSpeelTuin or 'noise playground' is also now under the same roof.

There are temporary exhibitions, conference facilities and a very impressive setting for the café-restaurant **Star Ferry**, overlooking the water. Whether the rather disparate collection of activities can settle down and give the Muziekgebouw a distinct identity of its own still remains to be seen. But as a building, it is certainly worth seeing.
Piet Heinkade 1.
Tel: (020) 788 2010;
www.muziekgebouw.nl.
Open (for telephone bookings):
Mon–Fri 1–5pm.
Tram: 25 & 26.

Muziektheater

The Muziektheater is part of the controversial modern Stopera development (*see* Stadhuis *in the* Destination guide *section, p78*) and is the home of the Netherlands Opera and the Dutch National Ballet. The performances of classics such as *Swan Lake* and *Sleeping Beauty* play to capacity audiences, so advance booking is advisable. Top visiting dance companies put in occasional guest performances of modern choreography. Musicians from the opera and ballet orchestras give free lunchtime concerts from September to May. Guided tours at noon on Saturdays for a nominal fee.
Tel: (020) 551 8103. Waterlooplein 22. Tel: (020) 625 5455; www. muziektheater.nl. Box office open: Mon– Sun 10am–6pm or start of performance; Sun 11.30am–6pm or start of performance. Tram: 9 or 14. Metro: Waterlooplein.

Open-air events

On summer Sunday afternoons it can seem that everyone in Amsterdam is heading for **Vondelpark**; the open-air theatre here is used for a very broad range of concerts, from traditional jazz to brass band music and even rock performances by home-grown bands such as Zuco 103. Between stage acts, there are buskers, jugglers, acrobats and puppeteers to watch. Check what is on at the VVV Amsterdam Tourist Office or just turn up and take pot luck.
Vondelpark: entrance from PC Hooftstraat. Vondelpark

Colourful modern art in the form of street graffiti decorates a small corner of Vondelpark, a green area renowned for its open-air theatre

Openluchttheater. Tel: (020) 673 1499. Tram: 1, 2, 3, 5 & 12.

Rock music

Escape

Big, centrally located disco, popular with visitors; live soul and hip-hop bands.

Rembrandtplein 11. Tel: (020) 622 1111; www.escape.nl. Open: Thur–Sun from 11pm. Tram: 4, 9 & 14.

Melkweg

Milky Way – located in an old dairy – was the last bastion of hippiedom until the late 1970s when the building was converted to a modern multimedia centre with a theatre, cinema, café, art gallery and concert hall, the latter specialising in world music, reggae, African, Latino and roots music, but also playing host to well-known British and US bands.

Melkweg is run as a cooperative and is informal and relaxed; there is no dress code, but regulars do turn up in imaginative party dress, especially for the popular Friday- and Saturday-night discos. Extensively remodelled in 2007.

Lijnbaansgracht 234A. Tel: (020) 531 8181; www.melkweg.nl. Open: Tue–Sun from 7.30pm. Disco open: Fri–Sat after the live acts, around 1am. Tram: 1, 2, 5, 7 & 10.

Paradiso

This rock venue, converted from a church, offers concerts from big-name bands who love the informal atmosphere and intimacy as a change from the impersonality of huge sports stadium venues. Like its near neighbour Melkweg, world music, reggae, African and Latin music all feature strongly. *Weteringschans 6–8. Tel: (020) 626 4521; www.paradiso.nl. Concerts from 8pm on various days; phone for details. Tickets at the door or from the VVV Amsterdam Tourist Office. Tram: 7 or 10.*

Theatre
Boom Chicago
This young comedy troupe now has a significant following in a small theatre on the Leidseplein. Different themes are featured in their madcap improvisational evenings, such as modern life and political incorrectness. Dine and drink before or during the shows. *Korte Leidsedwarsstraat 12. Tel: (020) 423 0101.*

Koninklijk Theater Carré
This former circus building is now the venue for big musical and theatrical productions touring from Britain and the USA, and long-standing favourites such as *Cats* and *Les Misérables*. The annual Christmas circus is still a highlight. *Amstel 115–125. Tel: Box office: (0900) 252 5255; www.theatercarre.nl. Box office open: daily 9am–9pm. Tram: 7 & 10.*

Stadsschouwburg
The Municipal Theatre is home to three Dutch theatrical companies that cover mainly the modern, timeless repertoire (Pinter, Albee) and contemporary productions. Until recently, the theatre used to host English-spoken productions, but at the moment (unless you understand Dutch) attending a performance is only advisable in June when the theatre is also a venue for Holland Festival theatre and dance performances. *Leidseplein 26. Tel: (020) 624 2311; www.ssba.nl. Box office open: Mon–Sat 10am–6pm; Sun 1½ hours before performance. Tram: 1, 2, 5, 7 & 10.*

The Municipal Theatre by night

Children

Amsterdam is a perfect city for children, who will enjoy canal trips, barrel organs, street buskers and riding the tram as much, if not more, than their parents. Most museums charge lower admission fees for children and will admit infants for free.

Favourite children's attractions in the city are the **Madame Tussaud Amsterdam** (*see p59*) and the **Van Gogh Museum** (*see pp82–3 & 90*). Two museums are specifically aimed at children: the **Tropenmusuem Junior** (*see p82*) allows them to learn about life in Africa or the Middle East by exploring implements, clothing, musical instruments and much more. The science centre **NEMO** (*see p64*) is full of push-button models that explain the wonders of holography, lasers, optical illusions, computers and cars. The big attraction for children at the **Nederlands Scheepvaart** (Maritime Museum) (*see pp62–3*) is the East Indiaman, the *Amsterdam*, moored by NEMO while the museum is under renovation until 2009. Tickets may be purchased at NEMO. Its narrow passages, staircases and hold can be explored without restriction. The **Aviodrome** at Lelystad airport provides the opportunity to play at being pilot in the cockpit of an airliner or to examine a space capsule.

The **Zoo** (Artis, *see p38*) is an absorbing place because it combines so many attractions: there are zoological and geological museums, a planetarium and an aquarium to explore as well as a big collection of wild animals and a smaller corner set up as a children's farm, where the rabbits and goats can be touched and stroked.

Amsterdam has several other children's farms which are not so crowded and which cost nothing to visit (though donations are welcomed). There is one in the Pijp district, **Kinderboerderij De Pijp** (*Lizzy Ansinghstraat 82; tel: (020) 664 8303; open: Mon–Fri 11am–5pm, Sat–Sun 1–5pm*). At the junction of Bickersgracht and Zandhoek, in the Western Islands (*see pp92–3*), you will find the **Dierencapel**, the Animal's Chapel, which is open during daylight hours; children can help with the feeding if they are there at the right time – usually around 4pm.

Cinema

Children who enjoy films will not be disappointed: several cinemas in Amsterdam have special children's matinées – check with individual cinemas for details.

Parks and playgrounds

Vondelpark (*see p71 & pp149–50*) is the most central of Amsterdam's green spaces; apart from the playground and the numerous ducks on the lake, there is plenty of free entertainment on summer weekends – acrobats, puppeteers and musicians. **Amsterdamse Bos** (*see p130*) can form the focus of a whole day's outing, beginning and ending with a ride on a veteran tram from the **Electrische Museumtramlijn** (*see p49*); the options here include cycling, swimming, boating and horse riding.

Swimming

The **Mirandabad complex** has an indoor subtropical pool with artificial beach, water slides, a wave machine and a whirlpool, and there is an outdoor pool as well for summer use. Very busy in summer.

De Mirandalaan 9. Tel: (020) 546 4444; www.mirandabad.nl.
Open: Mon–Fri 7am–10pm, Sat–Sun 10am–5pm. Admission charge.
Tram: 25. Bus: 15, 66 & 199.

Theatre

The **Circus Elleboog** may appeal to older children; this is a club which trains children in circus techniques – conjuring, clowning, juggling, unicycle riding and so on – but there are open sessions for all-comers on Saturday afternoons and all day Sunday, and the staff speak English. It is better to book places for your children in advance.

Passeerdersgracht 32.
Tel: (020) 626 9370.
Admission charge.
Tram: 7 & 10.

Scary crocs at the Zoo (Artis)

Sport and leisure

Amsterdammers are not great sports fanatics or fitness freaks, but there are numerous opportunities for working out or taking a relaxing sauna in the city centre. Most of the big sporting events take place outside Amsterdam but the venues are easily reached by public transport or by joining a special coach excursion.

PARTICIPATORY SPORTS
Health clubs
Club Sportive

Luxurious and central establishment with exercise gymnasium and sauna. Aerobics classes for all levels of fitness take place on weekdays at 6 and 7pm and other variable times.

Valkenburgerstraat 28. Tel: (020) 620 6631; www.clubsportive.nl.
Open: Mon–Fri 7am–11pm,
Sat–Sun 8am–7pm.
Tram: 7, 10, 16, 24 & 25.

Splash

An up-market and fashionable fitness centre which has all kinds of facilities including a weights room, exercise gym, Turkish bath, sauna and massage service, as well as aerobics classes throughout the day.

Looiersgracht 26. Tel: (020) 624 8404.
Open: Mon–Fri 7am–midnight,
Sat–Sun 8am–9pm.
Admission charge: a day pass allows free use of all the facilities.
Tram: 7 & 10.

Sports centres
Borchland Amstelborgh

Squash, tennis and badminton courts, and indoor bowling green all under one roof.

Borchlandweg 8–12.
Tel: (020) 563 3333. Open: daily 8am–11pm (deviations in opening hours are possible).
Admission charge: courts should be booked in advance; higher rates evenings and weekends.
Bus: 59 & 177. Metro: Strandvliet.

Squash
Squash City

Facilities include squash, fitness facilities, weight training, aerobics, solarium and sauna.

Katelmakerstraat 6.
Tel: (020) 626 7883; www.squashcity.nl.
Open: Mon–Fri 7am–10.30pm,
Sat–Sun 8.45am–7.30pm.
Admission charge: higher rates evenings & Sun.
Bus: 18 & 22.

Swimming
Marnixbad
Two pools in the brand-new Marnix Sports Centrum, in the middle of the city. In 2007, this popular swimming pool reopened as a modern sports complex in a glass structure, with two swimming pools, a sports hall, fitness and aerobic centre and café-restaurant.
Marnixstraat 9. Tel: (020) 625 4843; www.marnixbad.nl. Admission charge. Tram: 3 & 10.

Mirandabad
Popular, clean subtropical pool with wave machine, beach, water slide, whirlpool and outdoor pool in summer. Crowded in summer.
De Mirandalaan 9.
Tel: (020) 546 4444; www.mirandabad.nl. Open: Mon–Fri 7am–10pm, Sat–Sun 10am–5pm. Admission charge. Tram: 25. Bus: 15, 66 & 199.

Zuiderbad
This indoor pool was built in 1912. It still retains its tiled period interior and much of the old charm.
Hobbemastraat 26.
Tel: (020) 678 1390.

Open: Mon 7am–9pm, Tue–Fri 7am–10pm, Sat 8am–3.30pm, Sun 10am–3.30pm. Call as hours change per season. Admission charge Tram: 1, 2, 5, 16, 24 & 25.

Tennis
Sportcentrum Amstelpark
Fifteen indoor and 26 outdoor courts; free racket hire.
Koenenkade 8 (Amsterdamse Bos). Tel: (020) 301 0700; www.amstelpark.nl. Open: Mon–Fri 7am–midnight, Sat–Sun 8am–11pm. Hourly court fee. Bus: 170, 171 & 172.

Watersports
Sloterpark
Watersports centre on the Sloterplas lake with dinghies, windsurfing boards, canoes and wetsuits for hire.
Information centre: Osdorpplein 516–518. Tel: (020) 667 5900. Open: May–Oct, daily 8am–9pm. Hourly hire charge; deposit and identification required. Tram: 1 & 17.

Racing round the Zandvoort Circuit

The De Haagse equestrian event

SPECTATOR SPORTS
Equestrian sports

De Haagse Paardendagen, a two-day equestrian event, takes place in Den Haag (The Hague) in the second week in June (details from The Hague VVV Tourist Office, *tel: (0900) 340 3505*). Rotterdam hosts the biggest horse show of the year mid- or end-August (details from the Rotterdam VVV Tourist Office, *tel: (0900) 403 4065*). Amsterdam's own RAI exhibition centre is the venue for Jumping Amsterdam, four days of show-jumping competitions, mostly held end-November (details from the Amsterdam VVV Tourist Office, *tel: (0900) 400 4040*).

Football

Ajax, Amsterdam's home team, reached the peak of its success in the 1970s when it won three European Cup tournaments. Disgrace followed when the team was banned from European competition for a year because of the violent behaviour of its fans, and this was followed by a scandal involving underhand transfer deals.

Under new management the team has experienced a renaissance, winning the UEFA Cup in 1992 and the European Cup again in 1995. The fans are better behaved but matches against traditional rivals Feyenoord of Rotterdam, FC Den Haag, FC Utrecht or PSV Eindhoven are heavily policed as a precautionary measure. Ajax have a state-of-the-art stadium on the outskirts of the city. It hosts other sporting and entertainment events and has a museum dedicated to Ajax. Fans can be rowdy.

Amsterdam ArenA, ArenA Boulevard 1. Tel: (020) 311 1444; www.ajax.nl. Tours daily: noon, 2 & 4pm (also 11am Sat–Sun; more tours are offered when there is great interest). Ajax Museum & Fanshop. Tel: (020) 311 1685. Open: daily 9am–5pm. No tours. Museum closed on match days/events. Admission charge.

Golf

The **KLM Open Championship** takes place at the beach resort of Zandvoort, west of Amsterdam, end-August (details from the Netherlands Golf Federation; tel: (030) 242 6370; www.ngf.nl).

Hockey

The Wagener Stadium in Amsterdam is the home ground of the city's men's and women's teams and it is also used to stage international competitions. Nieuwe Kalfjeslaan 19. Information on www.knhb.nl. Matches: Sept–May Sun 12.45pm (women), 2.45pm (men). Free admission to league games, admission charge for internationals. Bus: 170, 171 & 172.

Motorsports

The **Zandvoort Circuit**, a short train ride from Amsterdam, has limited Formula 1 racing and there is also an exciting choice of international events held every weekend from July to November; details from Esso garages or tel: (023) 574 0750; www.circuit-zandvoort.nl

The big event of the year is the International **Netherlands Motorcycling TT Grand Prix**, which is held at Assen end-June. This popular event includes vintage, Formula 1 and sidecar races. Advance booking by post advised. TT Assen, PO Box 150, 9400 AD Assen. General information: Tel: (0592) 321 321.

Tennis

The **ABN-AMRO World Tennis Tournament** held in Rotterdam mid-February provides an excellent opportunity to see some of the world's top-seeded players in action. Information from the Rotterdam Ahoy Hallen. Tel: (0900) 235 2469.

Windsurfing

The challenging conditions of the North Sea make for good surfing: contests are held on various dates at Scheveningen, just outside Den Haag. It is a spectacular event. Details from The Hague VVV Tourist Office. Tel: (0900) 340 3505.

The official museum and fanshop of the Ajax club

Food and drink

You can eat the food of every nation somewhere in Amsterdam. The food ranges from American and Argentinian to Swiss, Thai and Turkish. Amsterdam has literally hundreds of very fine restaurants which serve every kind of cuisine that you would ever have wanted to sample, including some that you have probably never tried, such as Surinamese. The Indonesian kitchen is of course a must to try.

In addition, there are several gourmet shrines – top restaurants that have won Europe-wide acclaim for their inventiveness and quality, most of them French-inspired. These are inevitably expensive, but the majority of the city's restaurants are informal and inexpensive, though since the euro was adopted prices have increased dramatically.

Amsterdammers themselves do not like pretentiousness in any form and want to relax when they eat out. Restaurateurs have to fit in to survive, hence you will find that children are welcome in most restaurants and that there is nearly always a good vegetarian selection on the menu. Only the most expensive restaurants insist on jacket and tie, otherwise people dress as casually as they please. There is no pressure on diners to buy an expensive bottle of house wine; most local people prefer a cooling beer or mineral water instead. Another aspect of the easy-going attitude is that few restaurants have non-smoking areas, though

smoking will be banned in all Dutch cafés, restaurants, hotels and sports facilities from July 2008.

There should be no difficulty understanding the menus, which are printed in several languages; waiters will speak English, and often French and German as well. The menu prices include tax (17.5 per cent) and service (15 per cent) so there is no need to worry about hidden extras. Still, it is usual to give a tip, varying between 5 and 10 per cent – but only if you are satisfied with the service. Credit cards are accepted at more expensive restaurants. A number of the restaurants listed here are quite small, so it is advisable to book in advance for dinner, especially in summer and at weekends.

The following price indications are based on the cost of a three-course meal per person, excluding the price of drinks:

★	under €25
★★	from €30–50
★★★	from €55–70
★★★★	above €75

African
Kilimanjaro ★★
Small and friendly restaurant with pan-African cuisine – which offers the opportunity to choose dishes from the whole continent.
Rapenburgerplein 6.
Tel: (020) 622 3485.
Open: Tue–Sun 5–10pm.
Tram: 9 & 14.

Tjing Tjing ★★
Specialises in Dutch-South African cuisine, catering for special diets such as vegan and halal.
Cornelies Troostraat 56–58. Tel: (020) 676 0923.
Open: Thur–Sun 2pm–late.
Tram: 16, 24 & 25.

Argentinian
La Brasa ★★
The family that operates this excellent steakhouse prepares everything with care: from the chargrilled steaks to the steamed veg and salads. There are also other options, which include grilled chicken, fish and a spicy shrimp dish. Jacket potato included.
Haarlemmerdijk 16.
Tel: (020) 625 4438.
Open: daily 5–10pm.
Tram: 3, Bus: 18, 22 from Centraal Station.

Belgian
Chez Georges ★★★
Experience the art of dining out the whole evening, Belgian-style. Georges is in the kitchen off this miniature dining salon where each dish is prepared traditionally, from delicate fish to hearty game (in season).
Herenstraat 2 (Jordaan quarter).
Tel: (020) 626 3332.
Open: Mon–Tue, Thur–Sat 6–10pm.
Closed Wed & Sun.
Tram: 1, 2, 5, 13 & 17.

Unwinding at one of the many cafés

Dutch food and drink

Dutch food at its best means, primarily, absolutely fresh fish and seafood served very simply. Steamed mussels, filet of sole slightly sautéed, poached salmon, even lobster. The watery landscape of the Netherlands produces fresh and saltwater fish in abundance: prized mussels and oysters from the province of Zeeland, eels from the IJsselmeer, herrings and flatfish from the North Sea.

The place to eat fish is **Lucius**★★ (*Spuistraat 247; tel: (020) 624 1831; open: daily 5pm–midnight; tram: 1, 2 or 5*). This intimate bistro, with its white-tiled walls and tanks full of fish (not for eating), serves whatever is freshest. Try the *plateau de fruits de mer*. Fine wine by the glass.

Another atmospheric and popular fish restaurant is **Le Pêcheur**★★. Try their house speciality: smoked salmon, eel or tuna. Then order a lobster any way you like it. An elegant restaurant with attention to detail. *Reguliersdwarsstraat 32. Tel: (020) 624 3121; open: Mon–Fri lunch noon–3pm, Mon–Sat*

A herring stall

5.30–11pm. Closed Sun. Tram: 1, 2, 5 or 11.

For authentic Dutch food, head for the following restaurants.

d'Vijff Vlieghen ("Five Flies") ★★★/★★★★

This restaurant has become an institution over the years, with locals bringing their foreign guests to experience traditional Dutch cooking with a modern touch. They use local ingredients: from game and poultry to organic vegetables and herbs. It may be pricy, but the 17th-century ambience, complete with old tiles and a Rembrandt etching, is a memorable experience.

Spuistraat 294. Tel: (020) 530 4060. Open: daily 6–10pm.

Tram: 1, 2, 5.

Dorrius ★★/★★★

Just down the road from Centraal Station, this evergreen has been around since 1890, though now at a new location in two 17th-century buildings. Try the braised beef with cabbage, the 'hotchpotch' stew with meatballs and endive, stockfish, or hunter's hotpot.

It is not light cooking, but it is authentic Dutch fare. Start your evening off with an icy *jenever* (Dutch gin).

Nieuwezijds Voorburgwal 5. Tel: (020) 420 2224. Open: Mon–Sat 6–11pm. Closed Sun. Tram: 1, 2, 5, 13 & 17. Five-minute walk from Centraal Station.

For day-to-day Dutch specialities you do not have to eat formally. Fishmongers (*vishandels*) and herring stalls (*haringkarren*) sell tempting lunchtime snacks such as marinated herring, smoked eel, prawns or fresh salmon served in a bread roll. The traditional dish is raw fresh herring, best when the mild-tasting young fish (*nieuwe haring*) is available in spring.

Cafés and sandwich shops (*broodjeszaken*) sell filled rolls or open sandwiches stuffed with cheese, salami, salad and topped with fried eggs (*uitsmijters*). Equally Dutch are the fried food stalls (*frietkramen*), selling delicious chips with mayonnaise or spicy mincemeat balls called *frikadellen*.

When it comes to alcohol, Amsterdammers have a habit of combining their two national drinks – Pilsner-style beer and juniper-flavoured gin. The beer is drunk as a chaser to the gin, a combination aptly known as a *kopstoot*, a headbanger. Try gin on its own; *jonge jenever*, young gin, is an aromatic drink often combined with a mixer such as Coca-Cola. Such treatment would be sacrilegious, however, to *oude jenever*, old gin; this mellow, slightly sweet and creamy liquor, sipped ice-cold from a traditional stumpy glass, has its own distinctive flavour. It's usually served to the brim of the glass so you have to bow for the first sip.

Chinese

Dynasty ★★★

Very smart and fashionable, with a modern oriental decor of parasols, potted plants, silks and orchids. The food is highly original, based on the Cantonese tradition but combining elements of Thai, Vietnamese and Indonesian cuisine.
Reguliersdwarsstraat 30. Tel: (020) 626 8400. Open: daily 5.30–11pm. Tram: 1, 2 & 5.

Nam Tin ★★/★★★

This expansive Hong Kong-style restaurant attracts busloads of oriental tourists who come to feast on dim sum or dine family-style with dozens of dishes rotating and chopsticks clicking away. Don't be daunted by the menu, there are also pictures showing you what you can choose from.
Jodenbreestraat 11. Tel: (020) 639 2848. Open: daily noon–11pm. Tram: 9 & 14.

Sea Palace ★★★

This floating restaurant, moored in the northern docks, is popular as much for its riverside views and ambience as for its food. Excellent dim sum lunches are served from noon to 3.30pm and the most popular dinner dish is Peking Duck.
Oosterdokskade 8. Tel: (020) 626 4777. Open: daily noon–11pm. Next to Centraal Station.

The famed Sea Palace restaurant

French

Bordewijk ★★★★

This restaurant attracts many regular guests, and quite rightly so. Food and wines are excellent, the staff is well informed and helpful. It is advisable to book early. It gets noisy here.
Noordermarkt 7. Tel: (020) 624 3899. Open: Tue–Sun 6.30–10.30pm. Tram: 3 & 10.

1e Klas ★★

This café-cum-restaurant used to be Centraal Station's first-class waiting room, and its Art Deco fittings and wood panelling are reminiscent of the golden age of steam trains and cloche hats. Dine simply on a sandwich or bowl of soup or try the filet of sole and a glass of riesling.
Platform 2b, Centraal Station. Tel: (020) 625 0131. Open: daily 8.30am–11pm. Tram: 1, 2, 4, 5, 9, 13, 14, 16, 17, 24 & 25.

Beddington's ★★★★

Jean Beddington has been one of the city's most accomplished chefs for some time, and also the most unsung. English-born, trained in Japan, she has created her own low-profile oasis off the Utrechtsestraat. European or fusion? Don't label it, just book a table.

Utrechtsedwaarstraat 141 (5 minutes from Rembrandtplein).
Open: Tue–Sat 7–10.30pm.
Closed: Sun & Mon.
Tram: 4.

De Kas ★★★★

This greenhouse restaurant is off the beaten track in a park on the east side of town, and well worth a visit. Everything is freshly grown from the greenhouse and raised at local farms. Great wine selection and refined service.

Kamerlingh Onneslaan 3, Frankendael Park.
Tel: (020) 462 4562.
Open: Mon–Fri noon–2pm, Mon–Sat 6.30–10pm. Closed Sun.

Excelsior ★★★★

Elegant mirrored and chandeliered restaurant with panoramic views and terrace dining over the River Amstel. Seafood and game specialities as well as imaginative vegetarian dishes and a comprehensive wine list.

Hotel de l'Europe, Nieuwe Doelenstraat 2–8.
Tel: (020) 531 1705.
Open: daily 7–11am and 7–10.30pm, also Mon–Fri 12.30–2.30pm; booking essential; jacket and tie.
Tram: 4, 9, 14, 16, 24 & 25.

De Gouden Reael ★★★

Former café in the characterful Western Islands (*see* Unknown Amsterdam, *p93*), specialising in regional French cuisine, served with friendliness and flair. Inexpensive set menus. Terrace dining on the water in warm weather.

Zandhoek 14, Westerdok.
Tel: (020) 623 3883.
Open: daily noon– 10.30pm. Tram: 3.

Irresistible fruit pastries

Greek

Romios Greek Traiterie ★/★★

This modest takeaway in the Pijp quarter has a few tables for in-house dining. The Mezes are numerous and make a feast in themselves. Lemon chicken is excellent, as are stifado and moussaka.

Ceintuurbaan 350.
Tel: (020) 675 4324.
Open: Tue–Sat
noon–9pm. Closed Mon.
Tram: 3, 25.

Indian

Masala ★★

This unexpected restaurant serves up fiery vindaloos, and a soulful saag ghosh, as well as all the extras which go along with an Indian feast. Daily special is offered.

Spuistraat 54. Tel: (020)
624 0066.
Open: daily 5.30–11pm.
Tram: 1, 2, 5, 13 & 17.

Mayur ★★/★★★

One of the best Indian restaurants in Amsterdam, specialising in tandoori dishes. Friendly service.

Korte Leidsedwarsstraat
203. Tel: (020) 623 2142.
Open: daily 5–11.30pm.
Tram: 1, 2, 5, 7 & 10.

Moti Mahal ★★★

This fairly upmarket eatery is where many Indian businessmen dine while in town. Authentic, refined cuisine. From delicious onion bhajis to Kulma.

Nieuwezijds
Voorburgwal 34.
Tel: (020) 625 0330.
Open: daily 5.30–11pm.
Tram: 1, 2, 5, 13 & 17.

Indonesian

Amsterdam has numerous Indonesian restaurants, thanks to its colonial legacy, and Amsterdammers love this spicy cuisine as the antithesis to their own bland cooking. By far

Café with a streetside view

the majority of the restaurants serve a hybrid mixture of Indo-Chinese food, often further modified to appeal to Dutch taste. Far more authentic are the specialist restaurants listed below, often family-run and serving traditional regional dishes. Most offer a range of *rijsttafels* – set menus consisting of 15 to 45 different dishes served with rice and a fiery chilli sauce called *sambal*, best treated with caution. A simple *rijsttafel* of 15 dishes will provide a remarkably cheap meal of varying flavours and textures, while the more expensive versions usually feature a greater range of meat dishes – *saté*, beef *randang*, suckling pig, sweet-and-sour pork and mild curried chicken are typical.

Indonesian restaurant Cilubang

Kantjil & de Tijger ★/★★
This spacious restaurant offers simple Indonesian fare in a modern setting. Not too spicy, just the basic dishes like Nasi Rames, a mini-rijsttafel served on one plate.

Takeaway bar to the back of the restaurant.
Spuistraat 291.
Tel: (020) 620 0994.
Open: daily 5–11pm.
Tram: 1, 2 & 5.

Tempo Doeloe ★★★
The cuisine of this renowned restaurant is from the island of Celebes, where the residents favour hot dishes. Luckily, these dishes are clearly indicated on the menu and there are also milder options.

Utrechtsestraat 75.
Tel: (020) 625 6718.
Open: daily 6–11.30pm.
Tram: 4, 9 & 14.

Cilubang ★/★★
One of Amsterdam's best small Indonesian restaurants, a quiet and relaxing hideaway.
Runstraat 10.
Tel: (020) 626 9755.
Open: Tue–Sun 5–11pm.
Tram: 1, 2, 5, 7 & 10.

Sama Sebo ★★/★★★
Some of the best Indonesian food in Amsterdam. The first

Viva Mexico!

evening sitting (6pm) is popular with people going to the theatre or the Concertgebouw but is best avoided in favour of the second sitting (8pm) if you want to linger over your meal.
PC Hooftstraat 27.
Tel: (020) 662 8146.
Open: Mon–Sat noon–2pm, 6–10pm; booking essential.
Tram: 2, 3 & 5.

Sukasari ★★
Like dining at an Indonesian auntie's. Friendly staff serve authentic dishes, with excellent spicy variations. The *rijsttaffels* here are fairly priced and there is a vegetarian option.

Damstraat 26. Tel: (020) 624 0092. Open: Mon–Wed noon–9.30pm, Thur–Sat 5–10pm.
Tram: 4, 9, 16, 24 & 25.

Irish
The Tara ★
Irish breakfasts and other dishes, with music at night.
Rokin 85–89.
Tel: (020) 421 2654.
Open: food from 11am–9pm daily.
Tram: 4, 9, 14, 16, 24 & 25.

Italian
Segugio ★★★★
Culinary reviewers praised the achievements of this intimate Venetian-style restaurant. This makes it obligatory to make a reservation well in advance.
Utrechtsestraat 96.
Tel: (020) 330 1503.
Open: daily 6–11pm.
Tram: 4, 9 & 14.

Ristorante Caruso ★★
Spacious and stylishly furnished restaurant. Serves classic dishes.
Singel 550. Tel: (020) 623 8320. Open: daily from 8.30pm. Tram: 4, 9, 14, 16, 20, 24 & 25.

Porto Carrara ★
Authentic and lively pizzeria near Leidseplein.
Lange Leidsedwarsstraat 138. Tel: (020) 623 5672.
Tram: 1, 2 & 5.

Da Portare Via ★
Takeaway pizza is offered here exclusively, along with desserts and Italian beer, wine, mineral water and Prosecco. The authentic wood-burning oven is what attracts queues of happy locals and tourists. No phone, so just arrive and be patient.
Leliegracht 34.
Open: daily 5–10.30pm.
Tram: 13, 14 & 17.

Japanese
Sazanka Teppan Yaki/Yamazato ★★★
Two restaurants staffed by Japanese chefs who perform with enormous style and confidence, using ingredients flown in fresh from Japan daily. Lunch menus reasonably priced.
Hotel Okura, Ferdinand Bolstraat 333.
Tel: (020) 678 7450/678 7111.
Sazanka Teppan Yaki open: daily 6.30–10pm, Mon–Fri noon–2pm.

Jacket and tie required.
Yamazato open: daily
7.30–9.30am, noon–2pm,
6–9.30pm. Tram: 25.

Mexican
Pacifico ★★
Offshoot of London's
Café Pacifico, with
similar decor, but
smaller and packed at
weekends. Authentic
flavours washed down
by margaritas (visit
on Tuesday night for
cut-price drinks and
Thursdays for ribs –
one price for all you
can eat).
Warmoesstraat 31.
Tel: (020) 624 2911.
Open: Mon–Thur & Sun
5.30–10pm, Fri–Sat
5.30–11pm.
Booking advisable.
Tram: 4, 9, 14, 16, 20,
24 & 25.

Spanish
Centra ★
Centra serves authentic
tapas, paella and *zarzuela*
(fish stew) and has a
good selection of
Spanish wines.
Lange Niezel 29.
Tel: (020) 622 3050.
Open: daily 1.30–11pm.
Tram: 4, 9, 16, 24 & 25.

Surinamese
De Hapjeshoek ★
This takeout spot (with a
few tables) is a secret oasis
for locals who are
attracted to the salsa
music and spicy scents
emanating through this
Metro station. Try the
rotis with lamb, chicken or
veg, or the spicy noodles
and range of sandwiches.
Waterlooplein 6 (inside
the Metro station, east
side of street). No phone.
Open: daily 9am–9.30pm.
Tram: 9, 14, and Metro.

Swiss
Bern ★
Simple brown café
specialising in fondue
and peppered steaks. Two
sittings in the evening.
Book ahead.
Nieuwmarkt 9.
Tel: (020) 622 0034.
Open: daily 4pm–1am.
Metro: Nieuwmarkt.

Thai
Rakang ★★/★★★
A comprehensive menu
with adjacent takeout
shop.
Warmoesstraat 10.
Tel: (020) 620 9551.
Open: daily 6–10.30pm.
Tram: 7 & 10.

Vegetarian
All the restaurants listed
above serve vegetarian
dishes, either as part of
the menu or on request.
If, however, you have
special dietary
preferences, try one of
the following.
De Bolhoed ★
Hearty organic and
vegan dishes. Excellent-
value set-price menu
that changes daily.
Renowned for pastries
and banana-cream pie.
Prinsengracht 60.
Tel: (020) 626 1803.
Open: daily noon–10pm.
Tram: 13, 14 & 17.
De Waaghals ★
Organically produced
food and wine and vegan
dishes. Other dietary
requirements can be
catered for if you phone
in advance. Even non-
vegetarians will
appreciate the wide
choice on offer. It is
advisable not to bother
with the wine, though.
Frans Halsstraat 29.
Tel: (020) 679 9609.
Open: Tue–Sun
5–9.30pm. No credit
cards.
No-smoking area.
Tram: 16, 24 & 25.

Brown cafés

The *bruine kroegen*, or brown cafés, of Amsterdam are a uniquely Dutch institution. The typical features are wood-panelled walls and coffee-coloured ceilings, looking as if they have been stained by centuries of tobacco smoke. The wooden tables are sometimes covered in faded Persian rugs to soak up the spilt beer. Brown cafés are an alternative living room, home from home for the regular clientele, a warm place of refuge in winter when the big, pot-bellied stoves are lit and glowing, and the focus of much community activity. People come here for breakfast, morning coffee or an inexpensive lunch, to relax after work, read the paper, play chess, snooker or draughts, or just to chat with their friends.

Brown cafés are found on every street corner, but many of the most characterful are in the Jordaan district. **Café 't Smalle** (*Egelantiersgracht 12; tram: 13, 14 or 17*) is one of the oldest, originally founded in 1780 as the outlet of a gin distillery. It retains its 18th-century interior and stained-glass windows and serves spicy

This 17th-century former lock-keeper's house is home to a typical Amsterdam 'brown café', the Café de Sluyswacht

Brown cafés have an atmosphere of their own

Dutch apple cake to help soak up the beer.

On Spui (*tram: 1, 2, 4, 5, 9, 14, 16, 24 or 25*) you will find two very popular cafés next to each other. **Café Hoppe** (*Spui 18–20*), with its sawdust-covered floor, was founded in 1670 and is now very popular with trendy business executives, while **Café de Zwart** (*Spuistraat 334*) attracts writers. Their distinctions are often blurred in summer when the cafés spill out on to the sunny pavements to form one happy throng.

A variation on the brown café is the *proeflokaal*, or tasting house, where you can sample a very wide range of different beers, wines, gins, or liqueurs. One of the most atmospheric is **Wijnand Fockink**, tucked away off Dam Square at Pijlsteeg 31 (*tram: 4, 9, 14, 16, 24 or 25*). Another is **de Wildeman** (*Kolksteeg 3; tram: 1, 2, 4, 9, 13, 14, 16, 17, 24 or 25*), which always has 18 draught beers on tap, and 200 bottled ales.

A more recent phenomenon is the so-called white café – designer bars with high-tech interiors – such as **De Jaren** (*Nieuwe Doelenstraat 20; tram: 4, 9, 14, 16, 17, 24 or 25*). White is, however, too clinical a colour for the taste of many Amsterdammers who only feel really at home surrounded by the mellow patina of aged wood and the golden colours of a Rembrandt painting.

Hotels and accommodation

Although Amsterdam has a great number of hotels, it is also a popular tourist destination and has a thriving conference trade so advance booking is essential in the busiest seasons – Christmas and New Year, Easter and from the beginning of the bulb season in late March to the end of summer, mid-September.

One of the simplest ways to book accommodation is to use the **Netherlands Reservation Center**, or Nederlands Reserverings Centrum (Plantsoengracht 2, 1441 DE, Purmerend; *tel: (0299) 689 144; fax: (0299) 689 154; www.hotelres.nl*). Reservations can be made by email, telephone or fax – no personal callers. This free service covers the whole country and will save numerous phone calls. Hotels in the Netherlands are graded according to a star system, from the cheapest one-star establishments to five-star elegance. The classification is a useful guide, but tells you nothing about the character of the hotels.

In Amsterdam, the choice essentially falls into three categories: canalside hotels (price range from €125 to €185 for a double room), family-run hotels (price range from €90 to €150) and larger establishments (€175 upwards). Prices usually include breakfast, though VAT is added to the total bill. The main drawback of a centrally located hotel is

that these buildings are often protected monuments so the owners cannot put in modern facilities at will. Rooms may be small and the staircases are often steep, so the less-mobile visitor will have real problems, although in recent years some hotels have added lifts. On the plus side, many canalside hotels have attractive gardens and retain period details, and their proud owners also ensure that the rooms are appropriately furnished with antiques. There are several elegant purpose-built hotels in the Dam Square and station area which combine the benefits of centrality with a much greater range of facilities.

Many of the family-run hotels in Amsterdam are located in the Museum Quarter, Vondelpark district, and along some canals. Avoid the louche spots on the Damrak! Visitors must be sure to check the precise location before booking; do not trust descriptions that say '10 minutes from the centre'.

Hotels in the streets around the three big museums make an ideal base, but the further out you go into the Vondelpark district, the more remote you are from public transport.

Family-run hotels offer clean, basic accommodation at fairly reasonable prices. As with all but the most expensive hotels, breakfast is included, but too many hotels serve an unappetising buffet of cheap cooked meats, tasteless bread and lukewarm tea or coffee. Look for hotels that offer a better choice.

The larger hotel establishments dot the city, and they range from palatial Empire-style buildings with grand staircases and spacious balconied rooms to ultra-modern buildings, art galleries and huge atria. Most have the facilities you would expect of an international-class hotel – business centres, pools, shopping, valet parking and hairdressers.

If you are visiting Amsterdam on business, it may be worth sacrificing a central location for the greater convenience of a modern hotel on the edge of the city. The problems of driving and parking in Amsterdam are such that busy business executives do not like coming into the centre if they can avoid it. Most industries are located on the southern periphery and some hotels are to be found in the same area, close to the RAI exhibition centre and World Trade Centre.

★   under €60
★★   from €60–100
★★★   from €110–170
★★★★   above €170

Hotel Americain ★★★/★★★★

This elegant Art Deco monument was built in 1900 and has witnessed many of Amsterdam's celebrations on the lively Leidseplein across the way. *Leidsekade 97. Tel: (020) 556 3000. email: reservations@amsterdamamerican.com*

Hotel Mövenpick ★★★/★★★★

Opened in autumn 2006 in the new eastern docklands area (just east of Centraal Station) and next to the Passenger Ship Terminal, guests receive top service at this German chain. *Piet Heinkade 11. email: hotel.amsterdam@moevenpick.com*

Hotel Toren ★★/★★★

This hotel caters for business clients as well as families. Set on a picturesque canal in a 17th-century monument, it also has two other hotels in prime locations by the Vondelpark. With lift. *Keizersgracht 164. Tel: (020) 622 6352. email: info@hoteltoren.nl*

Hotel Nadia ★★

This hotel is minutes from Dam Square. Simple rooms, friendly service. Free internet and baggage room. *Raadhuisstraat 51. Tel: (020) 620 1550. Reservations via website: www.nadia.nl*

Hotel Hegra 269 ★/★★

A small family hotel on the canal where prices for the small, basically furnished rooms are still reasonable. Stairways are steep and there is no lift. *Herengracht. Tel: (020) 623 7877. Reservations via website: www.hegrahotel.com*

Practical guide

Arriving

Passports

All visitors must have a valid passport to visit the Netherlands for up to three months, but visas are needed by some countries, so check before travelling. Citizens of the EU, USA, Canada, Australia and NZ do not need visas.

Getting there

Amsterdam is easily reached by ferry or via the Channel Tunnel from the United Kingdom and by train or road from continental Europe. Even so, most visitors arrive by air, flying into Amsterdam Schiphol Airport, located 14km (9 miles) southwest of the city centre. This is one of the world's best and busiest airports, served by direct flights from most other international airports. Competition on these routes is such that you can nearly always find a cheap flight if you book far enough in advance and travel midweek.

Airport facilities

Schiphol is very efficient and you should clear the airport within 20 to 30 minutes of landing. There is a bureau de change in the arrivals hall as well as duty-free shopping, an accommodation booking desk and car rental facilities.

City Link

Schiphol train station is directly below the airport. You can access it from Schiphol Plaza close to the arrivals hall.

You can buy tickets from the ticket offices in the main hall or from the yellow ticket machines near the platforms. Trains depart several times an hour between 5.40am–1am and at hourly intervals in between. The fare is low and the journey to Amsterdam Centraal Station (CS) takes 20 minutes. Take this train if you are staying in the city centre. Board trains for Amsterdam Zuid/WTC or Amsterdam RAI only if you are staying in the World Trade Centre/RAI exhibition centre district in the southern suburbs. On arrival it is best to take a taxi from the station to the hotel until you have gained your bearings, though be aware that taxi drivers may overcharge you if your hotel is not that far.

Departing

Confirm your flight with the issuing airline 48 hours before departure (airline telephone numbers are listed in the *Amsterdam Yellow Pages*, or *Gouden Gids* directory). Check-in time at Schiphol is at least one-and-a-half hours before the scheduled flight time and two to three hours for international flights. There are excellent shopping and duty-free facilities at the airport – seeds, bulbs and floral bouquets are popular purchases but some countries do not allow the import of plant material; the knowledgeable florists will advise you. Check the Schiphol website for any travel updates (English) *www.schiphol.nl*

By train, ferry or coach

There are good, fast rail connections to Amsterdam from Brussels, Paris, Antwerp and Cologne, and from London (Eurostar – via the Channel Tunnel; change at Brussels). From London, boat/train services operate from Liverpool Street station via Harwich and the Hook of Holland. Ferry companies in the UK offer services from Harwich to the Hook of Holland, from Hull to Rotterdam and from Newcastle to IJmuiden, with train (bus from IJmuiden) connections from each ferry terminal to Amsterdam. Coach services depart from London's Victoria coach terminal. Details of all these services are available from travel agents and rail travel centres, but remember that the journey time can be anything from 7 to 15 hours and that it is often just as cheap to fly. The *Thomas Cook European Timetable* has details of these rail and ferry services, including night trains, and is available from Thomas Cook branches in the UK or by telephoning *00 44 1733 416477*.

Camping

The best-equipped and most central campsite is located on the southern edge of the Amsterdamse Bos, at Kleine Noordijk 1 (*tel: (020) 641 6868; www.campingamsterdamsebos.nl*), and is open from April to October. Using bus 170 or 171, it is a 30-minute journey to the city centre. Facilities include telephones, a shop, restaurant and bar, bicycles for hire, log cabins for rent and a lake for swimming.

Children

Children are generally welcomed and indulged. Some restaurants offer children's menus or children's portions at reduced prices. Children also pay reduced fares on public transport. Museums admit infants for free and, as a rule, children under 16 are admitted half price. Several museums offer discounted family tickets (two children and two adults), but the best deal for anyone planning to visit several museums is the I amsterdam Card (*see p180*).

Amsterdam Schiphol Airport

Climate

Amsterdam has a maritime climate
so it rarely suffers temperature
extremes. It is cold enough to freeze
the canals only once in every 10 to
15 years, though it can seem cold in
winter because strong winds increase
the chill factor, and fog blots out the
sunlight for days. In recent years, no
thanks to global warming, winters are
milder and so are the rest of the
seasons. Rain is unpredictable and
can be heavy in February and May,
July and November.

Conversion tables

See p175.
Amsterdam follows the Rest of Europe
system in many (but not all) clothes
and shoe sizes.

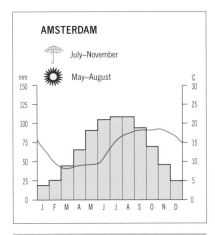

AMSTERDAM

July–November

May–August

**WEATHER CONVERSION
CHART**

25.4mm = 1 inch
°F = 1.8 × °C + 32

Possessions should be made safe and secure

Crime

Amsterdam's crime problem has been
greatly exaggerated, but even so, it is
essential to take precautions – most
victims of crime invite trouble by
carelessness or ill-advised behaviour.
Highly organised teams of pickpockets,
mainly from North Africa and South
America, operate in summer, preying
on tourists. Leave valuables in the hotel
safe or, if you must carry them, conceal
them in a body belt or something
similar and keep a tight hold on your
camera.

Be especially wary in crowded
shopping streets or on public transport
(the trains between Amsterdam and
Schiphol are notorious). Beware of
anyone who approaches you, no matter
how harmless their enquiry; they may
be distracting you while an accomplice
goes to work. You should also be careful

when giving money to buskers or beggars; there are people about watching to see where you keep your money.

After pickpocketing, car theft is the biggest category of crime. Never leave valuables in the car.

Mugging is less of a problem, but do not go out alone after dark anywhere where drug addicts, desperate for a fix, could attack you unseen; avoid parks, unlit and empty streets and the red-light district – and never try to take photographs in the red-light district; your camera could end up in the canal. If you are the victim of crime, you should file a statement with the nearest police station; it is unlikely that your property will be recovered, but you need an officially stamped copy of the statement to make an insurance claim.

Report the loss of your passport to your embassy or consulate (*see pp178–9*). Lost or stolen credit cards can be reported on the following 24-hour lines:

Eurocard/MasterCard
Tel: (030) 283 5555.
American Express *Tel: (020) 504 8000.*
Diners Club *Tel: (020) 557 3407.*
VISA *Tel: (020) 660 0611.*

Customs regulations

Personal possessions are not liable to duty but it is forbidden to import drugs, firearms or weapons (including knives). The current duty-free limits for the import of alcohol, tobacco, perfume

Practical guide

CONVERSION TABLE

FROM	TO	MULTIPLY BY
Inches	Centimetres	2.54
Feet	Metres	0.3048
Yards	Metres	0.9144
Miles	Kilometres	1.6090
Acres	Hectares	0.4047
Gallons	Litres	4.5460
Ounces	Grams	28.35
Pounds	Grams	453.6
Pounds	Kilograms	0.4536
Tons	Tonnes	1.0160

To convert back, for example from centimetres to inches, divide by the number in the third column.

MEN'S SUITS

UK	36	38	40	42	44	46	48
Rest of Europe	46	48	50	52	54	56	58
USA	36	38	40	42	44	46	48

DRESS SIZES

UK	8	10	12	14	16	18
France	36	38	40	42	44	46
Italy	38	40	42	44	46	48
Rest of Europe	34	36	38	40	42	44
USA	6	8	10	12	14	16

MEN'S SHIRTS

UK	14	14.5	15	15.5	16	16.5	17
Rest of Europe	36	37	38	39/40	41	42	43
USA	14	14.5	15	15.5	16	16.5	17

MEN'S SHOES

UK	7	7.5	8.5	9.5	10.5	11
Rest of Europe	41	42	43	44	45	46
USA	8	8.5	9.5	10.5	11.5	12

WOMEN'S SHOES

UK	4.5	5	5.5	6	6.5	7
Rest of Europe	38	38	39	39	40	41
USA	6	6.5	7	7.5	8	8.5

and cologne are posted at airports and ferry terminals, and because of increased security measures due to the threat of terrorism, rules continue to change, limiting the transport of common liquid items such as perfume and baby formula.

The allowances for importing goods duty- and tax-paid from other European Union nations are very generous. Stricter limits apply to goods bought in duty-free shops.

Cycling

Cycling in Amsterdam takes practice and courage, and the excellent tram system offers a far easier way of getting around. You may, however, wish to escape the city and explore nearby nature reserves (*see* Cycle Routes *on pp132–3*), and one of the easiest ways of doing that is to rent a bike and move out. These are the main places from where you can rent a bike in Amsterdam:

Bike City
Bloemgracht 68. Tel: (020) 626 3721.
Damstraat Rent a Bike
Damstraat 20–22. Tel: (020) 625 5029.
Holland Rent A Bike
Damrak 247. Tel: (020) 622 3207.
MacBike
Mr Visserplein 2. Tel: (020) 620 0985.
Weteringschans 2–4. Tel: (020) 620 0985.
Stationsplein 5. Tel: (020) 620 0985;
www.macbike.nl

To hire a bike you need to leave a deposit and show your passport or a credit card. It is best to hire a bike with conventional brakes and gearing: old-fashioned Dutch bikes have no gears or handbrakes and are stopped by back-pedalling.

Cycling is a common mode of transport both in the city and the countryside

You will be given advice on how to avoid theft of the bike, which you would be wise to heed. You will then have to cope with chaotic traffic and the wayward behaviour of pedestrians and other cyclists. Here is a tip: dismount at busy junctions and cross on foot until you have mastered the basic traffic rules.

Driving

Driving in Amsterdam is not recommended. The city already has too many cars, parking is difficult and expensive (you must always buy a ticket at parking boxes with a P) and cars are a favourite target of thieves. Instead, park your car outside the city centre and use public transport.

If you do drive to Amsterdam, choose a hotel with secure parking and leave your vehicle there for the duration of your stay.

Breakdown

If you are a member of an AIT-affiliated motoring association, you can use the services of the ANWB (Royal Dutch Touring Club) for free on production of an AIT Assistance Booklet (or ETI Booklet). For the emergency breakdown service, you can call from yellow roadside booths along major roads: *tel: (0800) 0888.*

If you are not covered by this scheme it might be worth joining the ANWB for the duration of your stay. You may contact the ANWB at Museumplein 5 or call

Trams are part of the landscape

tel: (020) 673 0844; open: Mon–Fri 9.30am–6pm, Sat 9.30am–5pm. Wegenwacht emergency service: (0800) 0888.

Car rental

Drivers who are over 21 years old and have at least a year's driving experience can hire a car on production of a valid licence, passport and credit card. The main rental agencies (*auto verhuur*) all have offices at Schiphol airport and at these city-centre addresses:
Avis *Nassaukade 380.*
Tel: (020) 683 6061.
Budget Rent a Car *Overtoom 121.*
Tel: (020) 612 6066.
Europcar *Overtoom 197.*
Tel: (020) 683 2123.
Hertz *Overtoom 333.*
Tel: (020) 612 2441.

Slightly less expensive are the following local firms:

Adams *Nassaukade 346.*
Tel: (020) 685 0111.
Amcar *Jacob Obrechtplein 13.*
Tel: (020) 662 4214.
Kuperus *Van der Madeweg 1.*
Tel: (020) 668 3311.

Chauffeur-driven cars

CS Limousine Services *Emmastraat 32.*
Tel: (020) 673 9045.
Van Delden Limousine Service
Berchvliet 13C. Tel: (020) 684 8408.

Documents

To enter the Netherlands with a car, you must carry the vehicle registration documents, proof of insurance (such as a Green Card), proof that the vehicle is roadworthy (an MOT certificate) and your driving licence. You must also affix an international identification disc to the rear of the car. If you belong to a motoring organisation, bring your AIT Assistance Booklet (or ETI Booklet) to make use of the AWNB breakdown services for free (*see p177*).

Rules of the road

Traffic drives on the right. Front seatbelts must be worn, and rear seatbelts if fitted. It is illegal to drive after drinking any alcohol. Maximum speeds are 120kph (75mph) or 100kph (62mph) on motorways (*autosnelweg*), 80kph (50mph) on main roads and 50kph (31mph) in built-up areas. Many residential areas have adopted traffic-calming schemes and laid down 'sleeping policemen' – raised ridges in the road identified by a sign showing a white house against a blue background – and in these zones it is illegal to drive faster than walking pace.

Parking

Apart from hotels, there is secure parking at Europarking (*Marnixstraat 250; tel: (0900) 446 6880*) and metered parking along the banks of the main canals – but space is difficult to find during office hours. Your car is likely to be clamped if you outstay the allotted time shown on the meter; the ticket affixed to the window will explain where and how to pay your fine. Cars parked illegally or dangerously are taken to the police car pound, and released only after payment of a substantial fine in cash.

Petrol

Only unleaded petrol is available in the Netherlands. However, 98-octane Super (not Super Plus) contains an additive, making it suitable for vehicles designed to run on leaded petrol.

Electricity

220 volts, continental 2-pin round-style plugs. Non-continental appliances need an adaptor; appliances running on less than 220 volts need a transformer.

Embassies and consulates

Most are located in Den Haag (The Hague); a comprehensive listing is given in the *Amsterdam Yellow Pages* directory.

Australia *Carnegielaan 4, Den Haag.*
Tel: (0800) 022 4794.
Canada *Sophialaan 7, Den Haag.*
Tel: (070) 311 1600.
Ireland *Dr Kuyperstraat 9, Den Haag.*
Tel: (070) 363 0993.
New Zealand *Eisenhowerlaan 77N,*
Den Haag. Tel: (070) 346 9324.
UK *Koningslaan 44, Amsterdam.*
Tel: (020) 676 4343.
USA *Museumplein 19, Amsterdam.*
Tel: (020) 575 5309.

Emergency telephone numbers
Police, fire and ambulance *112.*
Non-emergency Police (0900) 8844.

Health
If you need medical or dental treatment,
call the Tourist Medical Service on *(020)*
592 3434. This 24-hour line is
specifically geared to visitors and will
refer you to an appropriate doctor,
dentist, pharmacy or hospital.

All EU countries have reciprocal
arrangements for reclaiming the cost of
medical services. UK residents should
obtain the European Health Insurance
Card from any UK post office. However,
10 per cent of the cost of prescribed
medicines and all dental treatment must
be paid for. Travel insurance that
includes medical costs is still advised
and is essential for non-EU nationals.

Language
English is rapidly becoming the first
language of Amsterdam and virtually
everyone speaks it fluently. Signs are

written in English and Dutch, and
menus are printed in several languages,
so communication is rarely a problem.

Lost property
For items lost on trains: **NS Lost
Property Information** (*tel: (0900) 202
1163*; open: Mon–Fri 8am–8pm, Sat
8am–5pm). Items are kept for three
days, then forwarded to a central depot
in Utrecht. In Amsterdam, Centraal
Station; *tel: (020) 557 8544.*

For items lost on the bus, tram or
Metro system: **GVB Lost Property**
(*Prins Hendrikkade 108–114; tel: (0900)
8011 or (020) 460 5858; open: Mon–Fri
9am–4.30pm*).

Otherwise try **Police Lost Property**
(*Waterlooplein 11; tel: (020) 559 3005;
open: Mon–Fri 9.30am–3.30pm*).

Maps
Falkplan publishes a series of
comprehensive and up-to-date maps in
various formats: foldout, pocket book,
and a 'patent folded' version which is
almost impossible to use in windy
weather. These and other maps can be
purchased at bookshops and the VVV
Tourist Information Office.

Street graffiti

Media

If your hotel is linked into the cable network you can watch a wide range of TV programmes from all over Europe, including BBC1 and BBC2, French, German, Belgian and Italian stations, children's channels, non-stop pop videos and American news channel CNN.

Cable radio supplies BBC Radio 4, BBC World Service and Voice of America. Foreign newspapers and magazines are widely available on the day of publication.

Money matters

The Dutch unit of currency is the euro, written as €. The Netherlands shares the new currency with eleven European Union countries: Austria, Belgium, Finland, France, Germany, Greece, Ireland, Italy, Luxembourg, Portugal and Spain. Notes come in denominations of 5, 10, 20, 50, 100, 200 or 500 euros. The euro is subdivided into 100 cents. Coins come in values of 1, 2, 5, 10, 20 and 50 cents, and 1 and 2 euros.

Credit cards are accepted just about everywhere for higher-value purchases, as are traveller's cheques from recognised banks.

Money can be changed at banks and post offices. Amsterdam also has scores of bureaux de change at Centraal Station, around Dam Square and along Damrak. Some include a substantial commission. Hotels give you a poor rate.

Value Added Tax

BTW tax of 17.5 per cent is included in the price of most retail goods; so if you are a resident of a country outside the EU it makes sense to take advantage of the Tax-free for Tourists scheme when you make high-value purchases. All participating retailers will give you details of how to obtain a refund.

Museum and leisure discounts

Visitors will save a lot of money by investing in an I amsterdam Card (formerly known as the Amsterdam Pass). It includes free admission to more than 20 museums and attractions, the use of public transport and one free canal tour, plus 25 per cent discounts at many other attractions and restaurants. The holder will receive a free brochure which contains the details.

The pass is available from the VVV Amsterdam Tourist Office or Holland Tourist Information at Schiphol airport, or ask at your hotel. Three types are available: for 28, 48 or 72 hours.

National holidays

Businesses and shops are closed on the following days – although many shops now stay open on Good Friday. Museums are open, but for shorter hours, except on Christmas Day and New Year's Day.

1 January New Year's Day
March/April Good Friday
March/April Easter Monday
30 April Queen's Birthday
Variable in May Ascension Day

Variable in May Whit Monday
25 December Christmas Day
26 December Boxing Day.

Opening hours

Banks Normally open Monday to Friday 9am to 5pm. The Postbank, located in post offices, is open on Saturdays. The GWK in Amsterdam Centraal Station is open daily 8am to 10pm. There are ATM Cash points (Geldautomaat) throughout the city.

Shops Most shops are open from 9am to 6pm (5pm on Saturday), though some stay open until 10pm. There is late-night opening until 9pm on Thursday. Shops stay closed on Monday until 1pm (department stores 11am). Many shops are now open Sunday, usually from noon to 5pm.

Organised tours
Boat tours

Touring the canals of Amsterdam by boat is a must for a different perspective on the city. Tour operators usually supply taped commentaries in several languages to point out the various landmarks along the route.

Day cruises last around an hour and there are more expensive lunch and dinner cruises, at which food is served, lasting up to three hours. Day cruises depart at roughly 30-minute intervals from 9am to 6pm daily (services may be longer in summer and restricted in winter).

Reservations are required for lunch and dinner cruises, but even without bookings, you could just turn up at the landing stage. The main operators are:

Amsterdam displays its new motto in striking 3D lettering at the Museum Square

Canal Cruises

(across from Hard Rock Café)
Stadhouderskade 25. Tel: (020) 679
1370; www.canal-cruises.nl

Holland International

(in front of Centraal Station)
Prins Hendrikkade 33a.
Tel: (020) 622 7788.

Lovers

Opposite Prins Hendrikkade 25–27.
Tel: (020) 530 1090; www.lovers.nl

Meyer

Damrak, moorings 4 and 5.
Tel: (020) 623 4208.

Canal bikes

Make your own tour, get some exercise
and ride along the canals at your own
pace, pedalling at your leisure. Locations
are all over town; by the Leidseplein,
across from the Rijksmuseum, on the
Prinsengracht, between the Anne Frank
House and the Westerkok.
From Apr–Oct 10am–6pm. The hourly
price includes a map with five routes. A
deposit of €50 is required.

Coach tours

Scores of operators offer coach tours to
sights which are within an hour's drive
of Amsterdam, notably to the windmill
museum at Zaanse Schans, the bulb
fields and gardens of Lisse, the
IJsselmeer villages of Volendam,
Monnickendam and Marken, and the
cheese markets at Alkmaar and Gouda.

Tours can be booked at any hotel
through the VVV Tourist Information
Office. Caveat emptor: these tours are

A barge on the Oude Schans Canal

overpriced and overly long. You may
prefer to get a day pass to ride the train
or take a bus to these interesting sights
and towns.

Walking tours

Two organisations offer interesting
personalised walking tours of Amsterdam.
Advance booking is essential:

Archivisie Tours tailored to your
interests plus a regular programme of
architectural tours.
Tel: (020) 625 9123;
architectour@wish.net

Artifex makes cultural excursions for
those interested in art, architecture
and history.
Tel: (020) 620 8112; www.artifex.nu

Mee in Mokum Mokum is the Yiddish
name for Amsterdam; roughly

translated, it means 'the place where you feel at home'. The tours are led by knowledgeable insiders, many of whom have lived in the city all their lives. *Hartenstraat 16. Tel: (020) 625 1390. Each tour lasts three hours, starting 11am, Tue–Sun.*

Pharmacies

Chemists (*drogisterij*) sell all non-prescription drugs, such as aspirin, plus toiletries, personal hygiene products, tampons and condoms. They are open during normal shopping hours.

If you seek medical help and are given a prescription you will have to go to a pharmacy (*apotheek*) for medicines. These are normally open Monday to Friday 8/9am–5.30/6pm. Details of pharmacies open outside these hours are posted in all pharmacy windows and listed in the newspaper *Het Parool*. You can also phone the Central Medical Service on *(020) 592 3434* for advice.

Places of worship

Anglican *English Reformed Church (Engelsekerk), Begijnhof 48. Tel: (020) 624 9665.*
Roman Catholic *St John and St Ursula, Begijnhof 30. Tel: (020) 622 1918.*
Jewish (Reformed) *Jacob Soetendorpstraat 8. Tel: (020) 642 3562.*
Jewish (Orthodox) *Van der Boechorststraat 26. Tel: (020) 646 0046.*
Muslim *Kraaiennest 125. Tel: (020) 698 2526.*

A group enjoy a walking tour around the city

Police

In an emergency, telephone *112*. Otherwise, contact the Hoofdbureau Van Politie or Police Headquarters (*Elandsgracht 117; tel: (0900) 8844*) for help or advice.

Postal services

Stamps can be bought at many tobacconists and souvenir shops. The main post office is at Singel 250–256 (*tram: 1, 2, 5, 13, 14 or 17; open: Mon–Fri 9am–6pm, Thur till 8pm, Sat 10am–1.30pm*). Here you will find the full range of postal services, packaging materials on sale, a PostBank and express mail.

Poste restante mail should be addressed to the head office as follows:
Poste Restante, *Hoofdpostkantoor PTT, Singel 250–256, 1012 SJ Amsterdam, The Netherlands.* You will need your

passport as proof of identity to collect poste restante mail.

Public transport

Amsterdam has an excellent public transport system. A free information folder, with map, is available from the GVB (Amsterdam Transport Authority) office on Stationsplein, near the Metro entrance in the same building as the VVV. You can also buy tickets here.

The system is integrated, in the sense that the same tickets are valid for tram, bus and Metro. The simplest but most expensive way of getting around is to buy a flat-fare ticket (valid for one hour) from the bus or tram driver/conductor. Alternatively, you can buy rover tickets, valid for between one and nine days, allowing unlimited use of the system.

Generally, it is advisable to buy a strip of tickets (*strippenkaart*) sold in multiples of 15 at GVB ticket counters, post offices, Amsterdam tourist offices and tobacconists. Each ticket is valid for one hour's travel and you have to stamp one ticket for each zone you travel through, plus one.

In practice, most visitors are unlikely to travel beyond the Central Zone, so you will usually need to stamp two tickets for the journey. Fold the strip and insert the required number of units into the machines; these are located at the entrance to the Metro system or at the rear entrance doors on tram. On buses, the driver will stamp the tickets for you. Within the hour you can transfer to other buses, trams or the Metro so long as you stay within the same zone(s). Be aware that riding without a ticket can be costly. Transport security boards tram randomly and the fine is around €30.

Museumboot (Museumboat)

One of the most pleasant ways of travelling round Amsterdam is by the Museumboat (*tel: (020) 530 1090*). This departs every 30 (in summer) or 45 (in winter) minutes daily between 10am and 6.30pm from the landing stage opposite Amsterdam Centraal Station. With stops near 17 museums, it combines a canal trip with a museum visit. It makes twelve stops, calling at Prinsengracht, for the Anne Frankhuis, Theatremuseum and Woonboot-museum; Museum Kwartier (Museum Quarter), for the Rijksmuseum, Van Gogh Museum, Stedelijk Museum and Vondelpark; Bloemenmarkt (Flower Market), for the Bijbels Museum and Amsterdams Historisch Museum; Waterlooplein, for Museum Het Rembrandthuis, Joods Historisch Museum, Museum Willet Holthuysen and Artis Zoo; Nautisch Kwartier (Nautical Quarter), for the Nederlands Scheepvaartmuseum and Museumwerf 't Kromhout; and back to Centraal Station, for Madame Tussaud Amsterdam, Koninklijk Paleis and Museum Amstelkring.

Tickets, including day tickets giving museum discounts, can be bought from the VVV Amsterdam Tourist Office or at any landing stage.

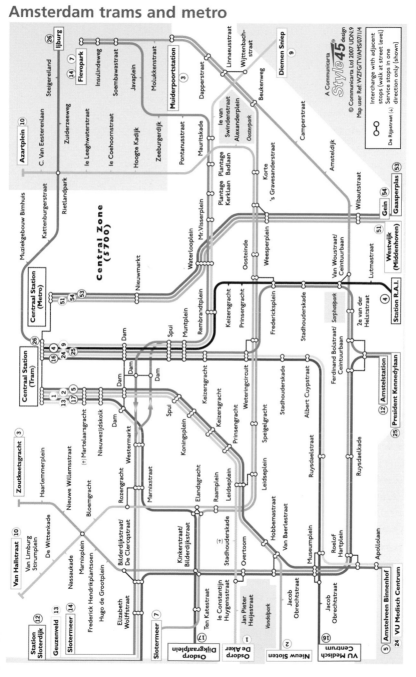

Night view of the Amsterdam Canals, Jordaan district

Taxis

In recent years, the taxi situation has become a disaster still needing to be improved. Strict rules became lenient and are now slowly being enforced again. Avoid taxi 'pirates' outside Centraal Station who will drive you out of the way and offer you off-the-meter fees that are often doubled. TCA, Taxi Chauffeurs Amsterdam, is currently the most reliable company. There are taxi stands around the city by Leidseplein, Rembrandtplein and the Dam. You cannot flag taxis down. Rates are slightly higher in the evening. Alternatively you can call the central taxi reservation number at *Taxicentrale* (*tel: (020) 677 7777*). The metered fare includes a service charge but it is customary to round the fare up to the nearest euro. An extra tip is always welcome for good service (10 per cent is a good rule of thumb).

Senior citizens

Pensioners from overseas should avail themselves of discounts offered at museums and other places (*see p180*) on production of proof of status (usually for ages 62 and older), but other discounts, on travel for example, are available only to Dutch citizens.

Student and youth travel

Students are entitled to discounts on museum entry charges and on Museumcards on production of a valid student identity card or other proof of age or status.

You can eat very cheaply at one of several large subsidised student canteens (called *mensae*), which anyone can use. The most central is Mensa Atrium, Oudezijds Achterburgwal 237 (*tel: (020) 525 3999. Open: Mon–Fri, lunch noon–2pm, dinner 3–7pm*).

Accommodation in so-called 'youth hostels' is available all over the city but prices vary greatly; you will often be approached by touts as you arrive at Amsterdam Centraal Station, and there are plenty of fly posters about, advertising their services.

They can provide perfectly adequate accommodation but you should check the cleanliness before paying and ensure that your room is not located over a noisy all-night bar. You will be expected to share bedrooms and bathroom facilities with complete strangers; so trust nobody and never leave your valuables unattended.

Sustainable tourism

Thomas Cook is a strong advocate of ethical and fairly traded tourism and believes that the travel experience should be as good for the places visited as it is for the people who visit them. That's why we firmly support The Travel Foundation, a charity that develops solutions to help improve and protect holiday destinations, their environment, traditions and culture. To find out what you can do to make a positive difference to the places you travel to and the people who live there, please visit *www.thetravelfoundation. org.uk*

Telephones

In all but the smaller, family-run hotels, telephones are found in every room as a standard facility. The hotel charges a mark-up on the normal call rate, so you may prefer to use your mobile phone for overseas calls.

Public phone boxes are not so easily found around the city due to mobile phone popularity. The existing boxes accept phonecards which can be purchased in various denominations from post offices and phone centres. Some boxes also take credit cards.

To make a call, lift the receiver, wait for the dialling tone and then insert your card. Wait till you hear a new higher tone and proceed to dial the number.

Codes

For overseas calls first dial 00 and wait for a new tone before dialling the country code (*31*) and the local code (omitting the initial *0*).

Some useful international telephone codes are listed here:

Australia *61*
Ireland *353*
New Zealand *64*
UK *44*
USA and Canada *1*

Traditional blue and white tiles

The code for Amsterdam is *020;* if you are dialling from abroad omit the initial zero.

Local Operator *(0800) 0101*
International Operator *(0800) 0410*
International Directory Enquiries *1888*
National Directory Enquiries *1888*

Phone centres and internet cafés

At some centres, you can make as many calls as you like and pay afterwards with cash, credit card, traveller's cheque or Eurocheque. You can send faxes and telexes, and purchase phonecards, too. A telephone card may also be obtained from the PTT post offices.

Time

Amsterdam observes Central European Time, which is one hour ahead of Greenwich Mean Time in winter and two hours ahead from late March to late October.

Tipping

A service charge is automatically included in the prices on restaurant menus and in metered taxi fares. Despite that, you are expected to tip about 5–10 per cent of the bill in a restaurant, and 10 per cent for a taxi ride – but do this only if you are satisfied with the service.

Toilets

Public urinals for men dot Amsterdam. Women may have to resort to buying a drink in a café in order to make use of their toilets. There are also clean facilities in museums, restaurants, cafés and department stores, which usually ask for a small fee.

Tourist information

The Netherlands has an excellent network of Tourist Information Offices where the standard of service is extremely high. Their official title is Vereniging Voor Vreemdelingenverkeer – the Association for Tourist Traffic – universally abbreviated to the initials VVV (pronounced *Fay Fay Fay*).

Offices are found near the station or main square in every town or city in the country. In Amsterdam the main office is located opposite Centraal Station (Stationsplein 10; *tel: (0900) 400 4040, for information at 55 cents per minute;* open daily 9am–5pm). This office provides a wide range of services in addition to information and advice. It also sells its own listings magazine, *What's On in Amsterdam*, a range of maps and leaflets, and it operates a bureau de change.

There is another office inside Centraal Station and branches at Leidseplein (all open daily). At Schiphol airport, Holland Tourist Information (open: daily 7am–10pm) is helpful for incoming visitors who require information and bookings. Outside the country, branches of The Netherlands Board of Tourism & Conventions can also be found in most capital cities: Some of the locations are given below:

Canada

*14 Glenmount Court, Whitby, Ontario
L1N 5M8.*

Tel: (905) 666 5960.

UK

*PO Box 30783, London WC2B 6DH.
Tel: (020) 7539 7950.*

USA

*355 Lexington Avenue, 19th Floor, New
York, NY 10017. Tel: (212) 370 7360.*

Travellers with disabilities

Steep hotel staircases and broken
pavements are the main hazards facing
travellers with disabilities. Aside from
this, Amsterdam has an enlightened
policy towards people with special
mobility requirements, and most
museums, cinemas and theatres have
ramp access and adapted toilets for
wheelchair users.

Brochures issued by the Netherlands
Board of Tourism and Conventions
and VVV Tourist Information Centres
give information that includes details
of hotels and tourist attractions
with disabled access and facilities.

In recent years, most of the tram fleet
has been replaced with new tram that
can accommodate wheelchairs. The
Metros are also wheelchair friendly and
there are lifts in all stations.

In Amsterdam, you can obtain
information or report a problem you
think needs addressing by contacting
the English-speaking staff of SGOA –
the Stichting Gehandicapten Overleg
Amsterdam (*Quellijnstraat 89; tel: (020)
577 7955; email: info@sgoa.nl; open:
Mon–Fri 9am–5pm*), an organisation
that works to improve facilities for
people with disabilities.

Amsterdam's waterfront tourist office

Index

Acknowledgements

Thomas Cook Publishing wishes to thank the following for the loan of the photographs reproduced in this book, to whom the copyright in the photographs belongs.

EDDY POSTHUMA DE BOER 11, 22, 33, 38, 44, 45, 46, 47, 48, 49, 51, 58, 62, 73, 74, 76, 77, 80, 93, 95, 98, 100, 101, 102, 103, 104, 105, 106, 109, 110, 114, 116, 117, 118, 123, 125, 126, 131, 134, 138b, 139a, 145, 156, 157, 160, 169, 179
FLICKR 13 (Jeroen), 63 (alex.ch), 113 (Matsuoka Kohei), 120 (Jack), 135 (Olga Khomitsevich), 140 (Travis Crawford), 153 (Anssi Koskinen), 155 (Hans Vink), 183 (majazmaja), 186 (Taz)
GASSAN DIAMONDS 144
MIKE GERRARD 138, 176
AMY HALL 7, 17, 23, 24, 25, 32, 34, 39, 73, 81, 83, 84, 129, 159, 168, 181
PICTURES COLOUR LIBRARY 61, 112
PLANET WARE 59
RIJKSMUSEUM 65, 67, 68, 69
WIKIMEDIA 15 (Dirk van der Made), 50 (SanderK), 90, 91 (Public domain images), 108 (Jaap Kramer), 121 (Romary)
WORLD PICTURES/PHOTOSHOT 1

The remaining pictures are held in the AA PHOTO LIBRARY and were taken by: KEN PATERSON with the exception of pages 35, 50b, 55, 78, 94, 137, 138a, 139b, 141, 148, 150, 162, 164, 165, 166, 173, 174, 177, 182, 188 which were taken by WYN VOSEY.

For CAMBRIDGE PUBLISHING MANAGEMENT LTD:
Project editor: LISA FIRTH
Typesetter: PAUL QUERIPEL
Proofreader: JAN McCANN

SEND YOUR THOUGHTS TO
BOOKS@THOMASCOOK.COM

We're committed to providing the very best up-to-date information in our travel guides and constantly strive to make them as useful as they can be. You can help us to improve future editions by letting us have your feedback. If you've made a wonderful discovery on your travels that we don't already feature, if you'd like to inform us about recent changes to anything that we do include, or if you simply want to let us know your thoughts about this guidebook and how we can make it even better – we'd love to hear from you.

Send us ideas, discoveries and recommendations today and then look out for your valuable input in the next edition of this title.

Emails to the above address, or letters to Travellers Series Editor, Thomas Cook Publishing, PO Box 227, Coningsby Road, Peterborough PE3 8SB, UK.

Please don't forget to let us know which title your feedback refers to!